A–Z

OF

WARRINGTON

PLACES - PEOPLE - HISTORY

Janice Hayes

AMBERLEY

First published 2019

Amberley Publishing
The Hill, Stroud, Gloucestershire, GL5 4EP
www.amberley-books.com

Copyright © Janice Hayes, 2019

The right of Janice Hayes to be identified as
the Author of this work has been asserted in
accordance with the Copyrights, Designs and
Patents Act 1988.

ISBN 978 1 4456 8453 6 (print)
ISBN 978 1 4456 8454 3 (ebook)

British Library Cataloguing in Publication Data.
A catalogue record for this book is available
from the British Library.

Typesetting by Aura Technology and Software
Services, India. Printed in Great Britain.

Contents

Introduction

Selecting key places, people and events which have shaped the story of Warrington is an almost impossible task for the town has changed drastically over its long history, and especially since local government reorganisation of 1974.

Appleton Bank Quay Barrow Hall Bewsey Birchwood Blackbrook Brook Acre Bruche Burtonwood Callands Chapelford Cinnamon Brow Croft Cuerdley Culcheth Dallam Fairfield Fearnhead Gemini Glazebury Gorse Covert Hatton Hood Manor Howley Hollins Green Houghton Green Hulme Kingswood Latchford Lingley Locking Stumps Longbarn Longford Lymm Martinscroft Oakwood Omega Orford Oughtrington Padgate Penketh Poplars Poulton Risley Rixton Statham Stockton Heath Stretton Thelwall Walton Westbrook Westy Whitecross Whittle Hall Wilderspool Winwick Woolston

An A–Z of the districts that make up present-day Warrington.

Until comparatively recently Warrington was a small Lancashire township north of the River Mersey which forms a natural regional boundary. However, even the course of the river has changed through time. Some areas to the south of the river have always been villages in Cheshire, whilst areas to the west, east and north were historically part of Lancashire or other neighbouring administrative areas. Some parts of present-day Warrington, such as Omega, are only just emerging whilst other districts in the west and east of the town were created as part of the Warrington New Town development in the late twentieth century. At the same time Warrington has been transformed from a town of heavy industry to a centre for technology and service industries and its population has effectively trebled in size.

In 1974 Warrington became part of Cheshire for administrative purposes before being granted unitary status in 1998 whilst technically remaining part of the County Palatine of Lancashire. So perhaps, not surprisingly, modern-day Warrington has something of an identity crisis. Many younger and more recent residents identify with Cheshire whilst older generations still recall the old Lancashire borough of Warrington of the early 1970s. The modern town is made up of former industrial or rural areas, long-established districts or recent communities as well as new residents from far and wide. Each of these communities could expect their story to feature in this volume, but even a brief outline of each district would take the whole book at the expense of the people who have helped shape Warrington's story.

Even choosing the people who should feature in this volume is problematic. Many figures were born in Warrington but achieved fame, or notoriety, in their careers in the wider world. Conversely others have fewer family connections with the locality but made their contribution to public life, science, literature, entertainment or sport while based here. Copyright issues also limited the availability of images illustrating the career of recent Warringtonians. Hard choices had to be made and so for the purposes of this volume there is greater concentration on more historic figures while those with more recent or ongoing contributions to the town's story can more easily be followed through social media or websites.

Warrington's strategic importance in the regional and national transport network has seen the town play a key part in national or world events, from the Industrial Revolution to numerous conflicts. This book is not a chronological story of these events but there are links between the individual sections which help to show Warrington's specific contributions. Equally the town has several unique, long-established traditions which add to the town's distinctiveness and deserve to be more widely understood and celebrated.

Finally, the format of an A–Z of the town needed some author's licence. Some letters of the alphabet had many candidates clamouring for inclusion while other more challenging letters such as X and Y required more ingenuity! Inevitably some readers will feel their locality or favourite personality has been excluded... so why not try to compile your own A–Z of Warrington?

A

The Academy

Eighteenth-century Warrington was a town on the rise, or as Daniel Defoe described it, 'a large, populous, old built town, but rich and full of good country tradesmen'. The River Mersey and the new canal network had linked Warrington to the key centres of Liverpool and Manchester and other growing towns of the Industrial Revolution. Warrington also became a centre of learning with ambitions to have a university to rival Oxford or Cambridge.

Between 1756 and 1786 Warrington Academy provided a university education for nonconformist scholars whose religion prevented them attending Oxford or Cambridge. The Revd John Seddon, minister of Cairo Street Chapel, was instrumental in founding the Academy, which was originally sited at Bridge Foot before moving to a new purpose-built campus in Academy Place off Buttermarket Street in 1762.

The original site of Warrington Academy at Bridge Foot.

The new Academy buildings at Academy Place opened in 1762.

At its height it attracted students from the West Indies and America as well as all parts of England (including John Wedgwood, son of the famous potter). The Academy had many distinguished tutors including leading scientist Joseph Priestley; Rheinhold Forster, a German naturalist who sailed with Captain Cook; and leading literary and classical figures including Dr Gilbert Wakefield and Dr Aikin, whose daughter became a distinguished author, more famous in her day than Wordsworth.

Joseph Priestley (1773–1804), probably the greatest eighteenth-century scientist, played a major role in establishing the Academy's reputation, although he went beyond its remit of producing more nonconformist clergy. He came to Warrington Academy in 1762 as a tutor of literature and ordained Presbyterian minister. Priestley was keenly interested in science and mathematics and reasoned that for his students to be equipped for the changing world of the Industrial Revolution the traditional classical education would not prepare engineers, industrialists and even politicians and military leaders. He pioneered a new curriculum for the Academy which provided a broad range of practical subjects rather than the traditional classics and theology. Priestley lectured on English, European, world and military history with other units devoted to everything from grammar to book-keeping and the tax system.

Priestley also pursued his own scientific interests, building a laboratory at the Academy where he experimented in chemistry, oxygen and the study of electricity, which led him to work with leading American scientist Benjamin Franklin. Priestley's work was rewarded with a Fellowship of the Royal Society and he was made a Doctor of Law by Edinburgh University. His educational influence probably helped encourage Arthur Bennett to suggest that Warrington was the 'Athens of the North', whilst Priestley's lifelong friend Anna Aikin described the Academy as the 'Nursery of Men'.

However, Priestley left the Academy in 1767 and by 1786 Warrington's early university experiment was at an end. The Academy moved first to Manchester and subsequently became Manchester College, Oxford. Little remains of its buildings with the original headquarters being winched up and moved to an adjacent site in 1981, before being almost completely rebuilt.

Above: The reconstructed and extended Academy building at Bridge Foot.

Left: Portrait of Joseph Priestley.

Anna Barbauld (née Aikin) (1743–1825)

When the Aikin family arrived in Warrington in 1756, fifteen-year-old Anna persuaded her father to let her continue studying classical and modern languages, at a time when a higher education was not available to women. Her brother John encouraged her literary talent and her first volume of poetry was published in 1773. Her poem in support of Corsican independence gained her recognition beyond the provinces, although it was assumed that this powerful work could only have been written by a man.

This is believed to be a portrait of
Anna Barbauld.

In 1774 she married Rochemont Barbauld, a former Academy scholar, and moved to Suffolk where he had a teaching post at Palgrave Academy. As the marriage was childless, she persuaded her brother to let them bring up his third child, a boy named Charles. As well as teaching the older boys everything from history to rhetoric Anna also wrote two tutorial guides called *Lessons for Children*. She advocated a series of simple lessons with a moral tone using repetition of concise facts about nature or essential life skills. These two volumes remained popular long after her other literary achievements were forgotten.

After 1774 Anna became a recognised figure in London's literary and artistic society, associating with Dr Samuel Johnson, Horace Walpole and Joshua Reynolds, the founder of the Royal Academy. She was adopted by the Blue Stocking Circle of academic women but was not a feminist writer, rather a woman who dared to campaign against slavery and in favour of American Independence – subjects judged to be the preserver of men. Initially she supported the French Revolutionaries and opposed Emperor Napoleon, but by 1811 she felt that Britain was misguided in continuing the war. She suffered a public backlash as her writing was judged unpatriotic and even treasonable.

By then her marriage had failed with her husband's growing insanity and eventual suicide. The new literary giants of Wordsworth and Coleridge turned against her and many of her works fell out of print after her death in 1825. More recently American feminist academics have championed the significant role she played in shaping intellectual ideas.

The Botelers of Bewsey

Today Bewsey is best known for its housing estate and former industries but it was formerly home to Warrington's Lords of the Manor, the Boteler family, whose coat of arms gave the town its blue and yellow link long before its rugby club was formed. This powerful family had moved from their wooden castle near the parish church to their lands in the royal forest of Burtonwood, making Bewsey the most powerful district in Warrington for over three centuries from the 1260s to 1586. As they spoke Norman French they called their new home *'un Beau See'*, meaning 'a Beautiful Place'.

The Knight's Tale

Warrington's too crowded... I'm off to Bewsey.

Its too misty and damp around the castle at Howley and the village is too noisy on market days now (although I make a lot of money from the traders).

I'm off to my hunting lodge in the forest of Burtonwood. It's a beautiful place (or a 'beau see', as we Norman knights call it).

I can still run my manor of Warrington from here but I can build a finer house than that drafty old castle.

William Boteler 1260-1280

A Boteler knight in his blue and gold coat of arms.

Bewsey Old Hall
c. 1830 with the
Georgian wing
on the right.

King Henry VII spent the night at the hall in 1495 on a visit to Lancashire. On the death of Edward Boteler in 1586 Bewsey passed to Robert Dudley, Queen Elizabeth's favourite, to pay off Edward's gambling debts. Dudley sold off the Boteler lands and Thomas Ireland, a wealthy lawyer, bought Bewsey and the manor of Warrington, moving in by 1602. In 1617 King James I stayed at Bewsey and knighted its new owner. The Ireland family owned Bewsey until 1675 but Sir Thomas's son was forced to sell off the manor of Warrington in 1625 to pay his debts. In 1675 Bewsey passed by inheritance to the Atherton family. They added a new wing in the mid-eighteenth century, where it was rumoured that Bonnie Prince Charlie stayed overnight on his attempt to recapture the English throne for the Stuart dynasty.

In 1797 the house passed by marriage to the Lilford family and Bewsey Old Hall's decline began. They demolished the eighteenth-century wing, built a new hall in the grounds in the 1860s and turned the Old Hall into two farmhouses let to tenants. Much of the old Bewsey Park was sold to Warrington Borough Council in 1926 as the site for a new housing estate. In 1974 Warrington New Town Development Corporation bought the remainder of the estate and more recently what remained of the building was developed as private apartments.

William Beamont (1797–1889)

Beamont was one of Warrington's most important nineteenth-century figures. As a lawyer and politician he helped shape the town's future whilst documenting its past as an amateur local historian. After an education at the Boteler Grammar School, he trained as a solicitor and set up his own practice in the building adjoining the historic Barley Mow overlooking the busy market place.

Beamont realised that Victorian Warrington was growing rapidly in size but had no proper water supply, sewers, street paving, refuse collection or street lighting and

William Beamont's mayoral portrait now hangs in Warrington Town Hall council chamber.

faced growing poverty, crime rates and poor housing. The police commissioners, made up of unelected wealthier townsmen, could no longer run the town properly.

In August 1846, acting on behalf of other leading local figures, Beamont sent a petition to Queen Victoria asking her to grant Warrington powers to set up a new elected body to govern the town. On 3 April 1847 Warrington received a royal charter with the Queen's official seal fixed at the bottom, which created the new borough. It detailed the town's boundaries within the counties of Lancashire and Cheshire. The new borough was to be governed by a mayor, twenty-seven councillors and nine aldermen elected to represent the town's five wards. They would serve a borough which had just under a tenth of the population of today's early twenty-first-century town and was much smaller in area.

The first elections were held on 1 June 1847 under the supervision of William Beamont, but only a small number of wealthy men were eligible to vote. By mid-July the new council had elected William Beamont as Warrington's first mayor and set up the first eight committees to run the town. Improvements to public health and sanitation were seen as a key priority after a series of major epidemics. In 1848 Beamont was instrumental in creating an additional Museum Committee which would see Warrington create the first public museum in the North West with a groundbreaking integral library.

After his mayoral year Beamont's contribution to local politics was recognised when he was made an alderman or elder statesman. He spent his retirement years as a suburban gentleman at Orford Hall documenting the early history of the town and its prominent families, aided by his professional career which had given him access to important family papers. He was very widely known and respected in historical circles throughout north-west England, especially for his *Annals of the Lords of Warrington*, which detailed the history of the Boteler family and their successors.

Arthur Bennett (1862–1931)

Bennett was a chartered accountant, local politician and author who had the vision to develop the town for future generations combined with a passion to preserve its heritage. He was the driving force behind the redevelopment of Bridge Street and the building of a new bridge over the Mersey at the turn of the twentieth century. His real passion lay in improving the environment and the lives of Warrington's inhabitants.

As in many industrial towns which had experienced a rapid growth in the second half of the nineteenth century, Warrington's workers found themselves crammed into insanitary courtyards off the main streets. Arthur Bennett was a disciple of Ebenezer Howard, who had a vision for garden suburbs with more spacious housing. Bennett had his own dream of a Warrington free from the pall of industrial smoke, where even the poor had good housing. In 1907 he set up the Warrington Garden Suburbs Company and planned extensive developments at Great Sankey and Grappenhall.

Although his ambitious scheme was never completed, as chair of the council's housing committee after the First World War he was able to realise his dreams. A promise to build 'Homes Fit for Heroes' was a key pledge of the 1918 Khaki Election

A formal portrait of Bennett with his distinctive moustache.

Bewsey Garden Suburbs prior to the opening in 1927.

and resulted in the 1919 Housing Act, which compelled local councils to build good houses and allowed them to borrow money to achieve this.

Under Bennett's influence Warrington Borough Council began to buy up land to build new council housing estates, beginning on a smaller scale with houses off King Edward Street before undertaking the more ambitious Bewsey Garden Suburb on land purchased from Lord Lilford. In July 1927, Alderman Bennett, the mayor of Warrington, officially opened Warrington's visionary council estate, which was designed with the needs of the new suburban community in mind with well-built houses, leisure facilities and schools.

Bennett also encouraged the council to provide parks as 'lungs for the people of Warrington', including St Elphin's and Orford. As some historic buildings had to give way to progress, he led the Warrington Society to mark their sites and significance with heritage plaques. He was also instrumental in ensuring that Warrington had memorials to those who had served in the First World War at land he provided at Padgate and at Warrington's main Cenotaph at Bridge Foot.

C

Coat of Arms

Coats of arms were the recognised means of identity in the frantic close combat of the medieval battlefield, where the unique pattern on each knight's protective shield distinguished friend from foe. Off the battlefield the shield formed the centrepiece of the coat of arms with a motto below it, a distinctive helmet above it and a crest and a mantle (cloak) on either side.

Local authorities later adopted a coat of arms, so when Warrington became a borough in 1847 its first mayor, William Beamont, helped create a simple badge inspired by the town's first Lord of the Manor, Paganus De Vilars. At the centre, lying on top of two flags bearing the emblems of Lancashire and Cheshire, was the De Vilars' shield, with six

Above left: Warrington's 1847 coat of arms designed by Beamont.

Above right: The new coat of arms adopted by Warrington in 1974.

upright red lions on ermine (white). Beneath this was Warrington's chosen Latin motto '*Deus Dat Incrementum*', literally meaning 'God giveth the increase', or God gives growth.

In 1897 Warrington became a County Borough with wider powers, and a formal coat of arms was approved by the College of Heralds. Beamont's simple design now had an additional blue border with eight closed gold cups representing the Boteler family, who had succeeded De Vilars as Lords of the Manor and completed by crested helmet, mantle and motto.

During local government reorganisation of 1974 Warrington adopted a new coat of arms to represent its historic associations with Lancashire and new administrative links with Cheshire.

The top portion of the new shield represents Cheshire with the black and silver arms of the 1st Earl of Chester, Hugh de Lupus (whose name meant wolf in Latin). On either side of the wolf's head are two gold wheat sheaves on a blue background representing former Cheshire districts now part of Warrington. Lancashire is represented on a gold bar across the centre of the shield with the red lion of Edmund, the 1st Earl of Lancaster, and red roses for former Lancashire districts incorporated into the new Warrington borough. The lower half of the shield keeps the borough's original De Vilars arms with the town's traditional motto below. A unicorn from the Boteler coat of arms stands as the helmet's crest bearing the sword of Cheshire in its forelegs.

Customs: Bawming the Thorn

Bawming the Thorn at Appleton, like Warrington's Walking Days, is an important local tradition which, apart from the costumes, has changed little through the ages. A reminder that holidays were once 'holy days', the ceremony takes place on or near St Peter's Day on 29 June but actually has links to a pre-Christian era when the spirits of trees were venerated and special trees were decorated, or 'bawmed', with strips of cloth. Appleton's tradition dates back to 1178 when Adam de Dutton, the local Lord of the Manor, planted a sprig of the Glastonbury Thorn Tree which was said to have originated from Christ's Crown of Thorns.

Over the centuries the tree and the tradition died out but were revived in 1880 to celebrate the marriage of Roland Egerton-Warburton of Arley and Appleton.

He commissioned a painting of the event by Robert Bateman, a Pre-Raphaelite artist and associate of Edward Burne Jones, and added a commemorative poem with the chorus:

> *Up with fresh garlands, this Midsummer morn,*
> *Up with red ribbons on Appleton Thorn,*
> *Come lasses and lads to the Thorn Tree today,*
> *To bawm it and shout as ye bawm it, hurray.*

Appleton Thorn or
Bawming the Thorn
by Ralph Bateman
(1842–1922).

Children Bawming
the Thorn in the early
twentieth century.

The tradition was revived again in 1973 and in the summer of 2013 children from Appleton Primary School danced round a much larger tree decorated with scarlet ribbons accompanied by a special fly past from a Spitfire to mark this fortieth anniversary.

Customs: Warrington Walking Day

Warrington Walking Day is a unique occasion when the town centre is brought to a halt on the morning of the Friday nearest the 1 July for a religious procession. This local tradition has its origins in the early nineteenth century at a time when religion played a much larger part in people's lives than today and Christian festivals were also a rare opportunity for a local holiday. In 1801 the first annual Sunday school procession was introduced in Manchester at Whitsuntide and by 1813 the idea of an outing for Sunday school children after the procession had become common in many North West mill towns.

Left: Reverend Horace Powys, Rector of Warrington.

Below: Warrington Walking Day in Wilson Patten Street *c.* 1900 by Thomas Hesketh.

Warrington's Walking Day was already established by 1834, possibly begun by the new rector of the parish, Horace Powys. At that time the procession took place in early to mid-June on the last Friday of the Newton race meeting, as a counter-attraction to the dangers of drunkenness and gambling. However, the town's main Walking Day has evolved over time, changing dates and routes and surviving declining church attendance, growing road traffic, changing work patterns and a multi-cultural society.

C

At first only the members of the Church of England (Anglicans) took part, but by the middle of nineteenth century there were three separate processions. The Anglican procession started from the Old Market Place (until 1873 when it began from the Town Hall.) The Roman Catholics had a separate route around the town centre after the Church of England parade. The Nonconformist churches also followed a separate route around the town which often finished at Bank Quay station for an afternoon out by train. Not surprisingly the processions often met head on in one of the main streets! The first time that all denominations walked the same route from the same starting point was as late as 1993 as a gesture of unity after the IRA bombing in Bridge Street.

The year 1897 saw a special Jubilee Walking Day to celebrate the sixtieth anniversary of Queen Victoria's accession to the throne. No less than 14,000 children took part and the procession passed the Town Hall steps where each child between the ages of three and fourteen received a small coin from the mayor. Further patriotic Walking Days took place at the end of both the First and Second World Wars to celebrate a return to normal life and the reinstatement of the annual event.

As well as the religious procession there has always been a carnival atmosphere on Walking Day, perhaps a reminder of Warrington's medieval Summer Fair, held from the 6–8 July. Walking Day became a whole day's holiday and excursions took place to the surrounding countryside in the afternoon after the walk. With the arrival of motor vehicles in the early twentieth century it was possible to travel further afield to the seaside fair at Southport. For many children who took part in either the main town Walking Day or one of the other district walks the real excitement was taking the Walking Day pennies collected during the procession to spend at the funfair in their local park. In the early twenty-first century it is increasingly hard to imagine the magic of one unique local day when everyone had a rare moment to dress in a new outfit and escape from everyday life.

Bands, banners, statues and new frocks are Walking Day traditions.

19

D

Warrington's Dinosaur

There was no one to complain when the first juggernaut rumbled through Warrington – but who would want to argue with a dinosaur? This first recorded visitor to the Warrington area was actually an ancestor of the dinosaurs and passed through Lymm and the nearby sandstone plains around 150 million years ago. No bones of this 3-metre-long creature have been discovered but it left imprinted into the original sandy desert a series of footprints the size of a human hand, which were later covered by a layer of siltstone. The resulting casts of the five-toed footprints were discovered in the 1830s at the infancy of the understanding of fossils and investigative science. The creature was originally named Cheirotherium, meaning hand beast (now usually spelled Chirotherium.) More recently it has been linked to a particular subspecies called Ticinosucus which resembles a crocodile. Warrington's 'dinosaur' would never have roamed a Jurassic Park as it belonged in the earlier Triassic Age, as a lizard-like ancestor called an archosaur. Its footprints can now be seen in Warrington Museum together with a half-size replica.

A half-size model of Chirotherium on show in Warrington Museum.

D

Charles Lutwidge Dodgson (1832–98)

Dodgson is better known by his pen name of Lewis Carroll and as the author of *Alice's Adventures in Wonderland* and *Through the Looking Glass,* and nonsense poems such as *The Hunting of the Snark* and *Jabberwocky.* He was also a lecturer in mathematics at Oxford University and a keen amateur photographer.

As he was born in Daresbury, which has never been part of Warrington, what is his connection to the town? He was born on 27 January 1832 at Daresbury parsonage, one of eleven children of the Revd Dodgson, who was rector of the parish. Gilbert Greenall was patron of the church and as Daresbury was part of the Greenall estate it has indirect connections to Warrington. Charles was educated at home and spent the first eleven years of his life in the relative seclusion of the parsonage, which he later described as:

> *An island farm...broad seas of corn,*
> *The happy spot where I was born.*

It has long been felt that Carroll was inspired by places and people he knew, with the Cheshire Cat in *Alice's Adventures in Wonderland* said to be linked to the carving of a cat on Grappenhall Church. However, there are many other potential local incidents that may have stuck in the subconscious mind of this impressionable young boy.

Alice meets the Dodo, who is said to represent Dodgson himself.

A view of the 1840 museum exhibition visited by the Dodgson family.

Could Alice's White Rabbit have been inspired by a legend of Bewsey Old Hall? Alice's adventures began when she chased a white rabbit down the passages of a rabbit hole. Around 1840 local historian James Kendrick wrote about 'a beautiful white rabbit which for time immemorial has visited the possessor of Bewsey and ... this timid wanderer... has been known to vanish ... leaving its pursuers to grasp the empty air'. Carroll's godfather, T. V. Bayne, was a friend of Kendrick and as headmaster of the Boteler Grammar School knew the Rector of Warrington who was the brother of the owner of Bewsey – so did Bayne recite the story to his godson?

Although this is speculation, we do know that in November 1840 the Dodgson family visited an exhibition which Bayne had helped to organise in Warrington Market Place. A bewildering collection of over 800 exhibits awaited the Dodgsons with paintings, models of machinery and manufactures, philosophical apparatus, specimens of natural history and objects of curiosity and interest.

Charles and his mother and father had their silhouette portraits done and then set off to look around. While the adults marvelled at paintings and Queen Victoria's autograph Carroll and Bayne's son could explore such delights as exotic foreign birds, including parrots and a dried human head. The strangest exhibit awaited them in the Philosophical and Apparatus Room where the Invisible Girl could be seen only at specified times – 'Curiouser and curiouser' as Carroll would later write in Alice's adventures! Could this optical illusion have been one of the inspirations for Alice's changing shape in her underground adventures?

The installation of Russell's Mad Hatter's Tea Party in 1984.

Shortly afterwards the Dodgson family moved to a new parish in Yorkshire. Charles's connection with the Warrington area was broken, although he did return briefly in the 1860s and took some photographs in the grounds of Walton Hall. However, it is fitting that today the popular granite sculpture of the Mad Hatter's Tea Party sits in the Old Market Place, opposite from the site of the 1840 exhibition. Designed by Edwin Russell and featuring characters from *Alice in Wonderland*, it was unveiled by Prince Charles and Princess Diana on 30 May 1984.

Entertainment

By the early 1900s Warrington had three professional theatre venues. The Royal Court Theatre in Rylands Street was a venue for popular dramas, variety acts and musical entertainment. Initially its main rival was a former musical hall known first as the Prince of Wales Theatre and later the Theatre Royal in Scotland Road. It was popularly known as the 'Blood Tub' because of the gory melodramas it staged. In 1907 a rival music hall appeared with the opening of the Hippodrome in Friar's Gate, but soon Warrington's theatres faced fierce competition from the silver screen with the opening of the Empire, Odeon and Ritz cinemas. Only the Royal Court continued as a theatre until 1960 and soon even cinema-going was under threat from television.

However, one Warrington entertainer's career had progressed from music hall to theatre, film and television as well as becoming a successful recording artist and royalty's favourite comedian. Wigan-born George Hoy Booth (1904–61) was better known by his stage name of George Formby and he became an honorary Warringtonian. From 1938 to 1944 he was Britain's biggest box office star with the screen persona of a shy, gormless Lancashire Lad. His risqué comic songs were accompanied by his trademark banjo-ukulele.

The Royal Court Theatre in Rylands Street in the early 1900s.

Above: The Palace and Hippodrome Theatre in Friars Gate *c.* 1910.

Right: George Formby portrayed with his trademark ukulele.

During the Second World War Formby entertained over three million allied troops, accompanied on tour by his formidable wife Beryl, who managed his career and potential love rivals with a firm hand.

When his film career waned in 1946 he embarked on several world tours, starred in a West End musical and appeared on television. He died on 6 March 1961, less than three months after Beryl and six weeks before his intended and controversial marriage to a much younger fiancée. Warrington came to a standstill for his funeral procession to Warrington cemetery where he was buried in the elaborate family grave.

Warrington Friary

From around 1260 to 1539 an important religious building called an Augustinian Friary occupied land near Bridge Foot stretching westward from Bridge Street. Austin friars were members of a religious order that followed the teachings of St Augustine and took their name from the Latin word '*frater*', meaning 'brother'. Whilst monks lived apart from the rest of the world, friars worked amongst the ordinary townspeople, preaching and teaching the Christian faith and caring for the sick in their hospital. Friars were forbidden to own possessions and so had to rely on the support of wealthy local families such as the Botelers.

Warrington Bridge and the tower of the Friary (left) in the 1580s.

The Friary was sited close to the three-arched bridge over the River Mersey, on the route of anyone visiting Warrington's busy market and convenient for the many pilgrims who came to hear the friars preach. Warrington's Friary had an added importance in the early 1480s as the Augustinian order in England and Ireland was headed by the local figure of Thomas Penketh, one of the most respected religious scholars of his day. Honours at Oxford University led in 1474 to a professorship of Theology at Padua where he published several early printed books. On his return to England he became embroiled in the turmoil surrounding Richard III's seizure of the throne from his nephew, young King Edward V. William Shakespeare's dramatisation of events would later give Friar Penketh a key role in legitimising Richard's succession.

Penketh's sermon in support of Richard III at Easter in 1484 was said to have brought disgrace to himself and his Order, but it was actually King Henry VIII's later break with the Roman Catholic Church which led to the Friary's closure in 1539. All religious houses were closed and Warrington Friary's property was sold off to Thomas Holcroft, 'with all its houses, buildings, barns, stables, dove houses, orchards, gardens, lands, grounds.... and a three acre field called White Meadow'.

The Friary Church was renamed the Jesus Church and continued in use until it was probably destroyed in 1643 by the Parliamentarians during the Civil War against King Charles I. Building stone was too good to waste and part of it was reused in the lord of the manor's courthouse in the Market Place (now Golden Square).

Anyone visiting Bridge Street today would find it hard to believe that such an important building ever existed, although the street names of Friars Gate and St Austin's Lane give a clue to the site of the Friary. More evidence has been unearthed by archaeologists who excavated the site in 1887, 1931, 1978 and 1998, revealing that the building and its surrounding lands stretched as far as Warrington Museum where many of their finds are now displayed. Discoveries at another Augustinian site at Norton Priory give an even more complete picture of life at Warrington's Friary.

Excavations in the 1880s revealed the Friary's foundation walls and tiled floor.

Fairs and Markets

As a focus of the regional river and road transport network, Warrington was ideally placed to develop as a site for fairs and markets. Fairs usually took place on saints' days and provided opportunities for trading and amusements. Warrington gained the right to hold fairs in 1255 and 1288 with a summer fair held in early July starting on the Eve of St Thomas's Day and a winter fair starting on 30 November, the Eve of St Andrew's Day. Each fair lasted for eight days and was centred on the Corn Market or Old Market Place (later known as Golden Square.)

William Beamont recalled the associated traditions:

> The formal opening of the fair was preceded by a procession, at the head of which marched the Town Crier...Behind him some of the leading persons of the town, with the four manor constables and their deputy, while the Steward of the Lord of the Manor closed the procession, which halted at various accustomed places, where the Steward, after the usual cry of "Oh Yes," made three times by the Town Crier, read out in a loud voice a quaint old proclamation.... to warn all persons attending the fair, to beware of all knavery, and unfair dealing, and warning all idlers, vagrants, and vagabonds to depart.

> No sooner was the fair declared to be open than the Corn Market and the streets adjoining it were filled with cows of all sorts and ages, ranging along the streets in rows...and so great was the crowd that extreme care was needed to go through it with safety. The next day when horses were to be sold, the crowd was great or greater still.

Warrington's Bellman or Town Crier in his blue and red livery.

Probably Warrington's last horse fair in Winwick Street in the early twentieth century.

The Corn Market was filled with wooden stalls selling broadcloth from the west of England, cloth from Yorkshire, Welsh flannels and knitted stockings, cutlery and hardware from Sheffield and Birmingham, linens from Ireland, and toys, food, confectionery and sweetmeats from far and wide. Beamont also recalled the entertainment to attract the crowds:

Caravans came in numbers to show dwarfs no bigger than Tom Thumb and giants, as their possessors said measuring twelve feet high... and there were stuffed mermaids.

The noise and hubbub and the shouts of the showmen continued throughout the fair ...and to these were added the continuous blare of brazen trumpets, the clashing of cymbals and the beating of drums.

There was also an annual Whitsuntide fair held in Church Street with stalls called 'standings', swingboats and peep shows on the south of the street. Victorian morality felt the fair caused 'scenes of riot and dissipation which were a disgrace to the age and country' and banned it after 1859. The two annual fairs had also disappeared before the First World War but Warrington's weekly markets continued.

The royal market charter granted to the Boteler's in 1277 probably confirmed the existence of a well-established event. The market had originated in Church Street, near to the site of the ford and their castle, but with the building of Warrington Bridge the focus of the town and the market moved to the busy junction of north-south and east-west traffic which became known as Market Gate.

By the 1840s Warrington Market Place had become a focus for country people trading grain, vegetables and meat at the weekly markets and also livestock at the fortnightly Wednesday fairs. Dairy produce such as farm fresh butter and cheese was also on offer at the temporary trestle tables in front of the Barley Mow Inn.

In 1856 a covered market hall with attached shed was erected in the centre of the market place and as trade increased a second general market was added behind the Barley Mow in the 1880s. As part of the town centre regeneration of the late twentieth century the whole market was relocated to a new Bank Street site in 1974 with only the former cast iron Fish Market structure remaining. At the completion of the Time Square development a replacement market site will front onto Bridge Street whilst the Old Market site still provides entertainment at the heart of the Golden Square shopping centre.

Left: Church Street fair photographed by Samuel Mather Webster in 1856.

Below: Warrington's market in the 1840s in front of the Barley Mow Inn.

G

Golden Gates

The stunning golden gates that enhance Warrington's Grade I listed Town Hall are a fitting symbol of the town's role as the gateway to the region. However, while its gates may be golden, the building itself has copper foundations. It was built by Thomas Patten, whose father had seen the importance of developing Warrington's links with the port of Liverpool by improving the passage of ships up the Mersey to Bank Quay. The Pattens also began smelting Cornish copper at their wharf at Bank Quay.

But there was a sinister side to the Patten's new-found fortunes: it was partly dependent on the infamous slave trade. The copper works produced the bangles,

Warrington's Golden Gates now frame the Town Hall from Sankey Street.

Above: This 1772 view shows the Town Hall on a raised bank (left).

Left: Portrait of Thomas Patten by Hamlet Winstanley (now at Warrington Museum).

which were used as currency to purchase slaves in Africa and large vessels needed to boil sugar and distil rum on the West Indian plantations.

Thomas Patten continued to increase the family fortunes and had ambitions to join the landed gentry. He had his portrait painted by well-known artist Hamlet Winstanley, which shows him wearing a fine gold velvet coat and sitting at an ornate desk, with his hands upon numerous business documents.

In 1750 he commissioned a fine new mansion overlooking his copper works from leading architect James Gibbs, best known for the London church of St Martin's-in-the-Field in Trafalgar Square and the Radcliffe Library in Oxford. Copper waste from Patten's works was moulded into blocks used for Bank House's foundations, floors and cellar walls. The ground-floor window frames were also made from copper while the interior had a grand staircase and finely moulded plasterwork provided by Gibb's team of Italian craftsmen.

This postcard view of *c*. 1901 shows the Walker Fountain behind the gates.

By the 1870s Patten's descendants had risen in status and preferred to live in their mansion at Winmarleigh near Preston. As Warrington needed a much larger town hall Bank Hall and its grounds were purchased with subsidies from the Patten and Crosfield families. There were soon complaints that the building was hidden from public view by a high brick wall, so local councillor and ironmaster Frederick Monks purchased ornate gates as a replacement.

These grand gates were originally designed by the Coalbrookdale Iron Works for the International Exhibition of 1862, and potentially for the planned new royal residence at Sandringham in Norfolk. Unfortunately, Queen Victoria was diverted from their trade stand at the exhibition, as clearly visible through the gates was a statue of Oliver Cromwell, a man detested by the royal family as an enemy of King Charles I.

Coalbrookdale found it difficult to sell gates on this scale and Monks was able to acquire them for the town. The central Prince of Wales motif above the centre arch was replaced with Warrington's coat of arms but the gates remained painted black. On Warrington's annual Walking Day in 1895 Monks ceremoniously opened the gates with a golden key to allow the assembled churches to set off on their procession.

In May 1900 an ornamental cast-iron fountain was sited behind the gates in honour of Peter Walker, founder of Walker's Brewery. It was manufactured by Walter Mcfarlane & Company of Possil Park, Glasgow, and had a 40-foot ground basin. It hid the Town Hall from view and on windy days drenched passers-by in Winmarleigh Street until it was demolished for scrap metal as a patriotic wartime gesture in March 1942.

The gates were finally decorated in their royal colours in celebration of Queen Elizabeth's Silver Jubilee of 1977. In late 2018 they were dismantled for a full restoration to ensure they remain a glowing symbol of Warrington's heritage.

Howley

Today this area of Warrington is officially known as Fairfield and Howley but Howley itself was the earliest settlement in central Warrington sited on the north side of the ford from Latchford used from Prehistoric times. Howley traditionally means a marshy meadow or lea in the hollow of a river bend.

When William Duke of Normandy conquered England in 1066 there was already a small fortified village at Howley. The Domesday Survey of 1086 describes the whole area as the manor of 'Walintune' and mentions the church of St Elphin, which had probably existed since the seventh century.

The Villager's Tale

Life's hard in medieval Warrington ... especially for us ordinary people, the villeins (or villagers as you'd call us).

We spend our days working in the fields of Howley, growing food for our families and looking after our animals.
We have to work for the lord of the Manor too. Those Botelers own us!
We can't even leave the village in search of a better life. It's alright for them, snug in their castle on Mote Hill!

Warrington villager c1260

Medieval villagers hard at work ploughing the open fields around Howley.

King William shared out his new lands amongst loyal Norman knights to govern for him. Firstly Paganus de Vilars and later his descendants the Boteler family ruled Warrington. By 1200 Warrington had become a small town centred on its wooden castle at Mote Hill next to the church. The cottages along Church Street were home to the villagers who worked the open fields in Howley.

In the mid-thirteenth century the Botelers moved to Bewsey. By 1290 the town centre had moved to the 'New Street' (Bridge Street) leading to Warrington's new bridge, which replaced the ford as the river crossing. Bustling weekly markets that were first held in Church Street moved to the crossroads at Market Gate. St Elphin's remained as Warrington's parish church and the heart of local government.

In the early twelfth century the church was rebuilt in stone and remodelled in the fourteenth century as the town grew in prosperity. The crypt of this building and its staircase, the main chancel and parts of the transept survived the drastic remodelling of the Victorian period. The church was used as a Royalist stronghold during the attack from the Parliamentary army in the siege of 1643 during the Civil War. By the

St Elphin's Church and its dominant spire seen from Church Street.

eighteenth century many of the wealthier families lived at the opposite side of the town and funded the building of Holy Trinity Church, allowing St Elphin's to deteriorate.

The arrival of the Revd William Quekett in 1854 as rector of Warrington led to its virtual rebuilding with the addition of a new spire which soared over the landscape at a height of around 281 feet (85.65 metres), making it the third highest parish church spire in England. Much of Warrington's history is still visible through the church's memorials and stained-glass windows.

Meanwhile Howley became an industrial area and although the outline of the old village surrounded by open fields was still evident on Hall's map of 1826 tanneries and Ryland's wireworks had already appeared, with Warrington's Workhouse on the town side of Church Street. Howley and its newer neighbour of Fairfield were filled with rows of terraced housing for the workers.

Soon the only open space was the grounds of Warrington Training College and former Clergy Daughter's School beside the parish church. One of the Clergy Daughters was Richmal Crompton, better known as the author of *Just William*. She later recalled boarding school life not unlike that of Hogwarts!

> My chief memory is one of dark corridors and narrow mysterious passages. In the Lower School we peopled every corner of it with ghosts. ...There was the narrow passage that led from the Sixth Form room, past the top of the cloakroom steps, to the ante room, where a pair of mysterious hands were supposed to chase their victims at night.

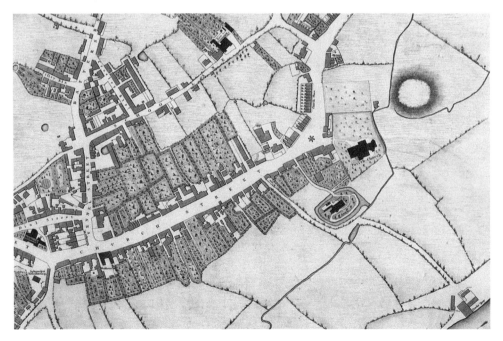

Hall's 1826 map still shows Howley's castle site and medieval village pattern.

Above: The former Ryland's wireworks site seen from the parish church spire.

Below: The Clergy Daughters' School next to the parish church, early 1900s.

The school moved to Darley Dale in 1907 and the college was gutted by a devastating fire on 28 December 1923, but St Katherine's Chapel survived as a community centre and its grounds became St Elphin's Park. By the beginning of the twenty-first century the wire works and tanneries were gone together with many of the old terraces, but Fairfield and Howley retain their strong sense of community and heritage.

John Howard (1726–90)

In the late eighteenth century Warrington became linked to noted social reformer John Howard during his campaign to improve conditions for prisoners. As High Sheriff of Bedfordshire Howard had been shocked at the conditions he found in the county's jails and began to lobby parliament for reforms to the penal system. He travelled over 42,000 miles on a fact-finding tour of English and European jails including a visit to Warrington's jail attached to the Church Street Workhouse.

In search of a publisher for his series of works including *The State of the Prisons in England and Wales*, he chose the well-regarded firm of William Eyres Press in Horsemarket Street. As Eyres was both his editor as well as printer, Howard lodged at a silversmith's shop nearby in Bridge Street in the 1770s and 1780s.

Howard's links to Warrington were commemorated in the redevelopment of Bridge Street in the early 1900s, although his former lodgings disappeared. In its place rose a new building with terracotta reliefs showing Howard helping to free prisoners from some of the harsher conditions they endured. A plaque marking his stay in Warrington was commissioned by the Warrington Society. The unveiling ceremony took place on 5 April 1907, the 130th anniversary of the publication of Howard's work. The building's handsome façade will adorn the linking structure between Bridge Street and the Time Square development scheduled for completion by 2021.

Portrait medallion of John Howard, prison reformer.

I

Industrial Warrington

Location, location, location has been the key to Warrington's prosperity and the development of its industries. By the end of the eighteenth century Warrington's developing port had been linked with the canal network, opening up access to the Cheshire salt fields and linking Warrington to the nearby collieries. By the 1870s Warrington had water and rail networks for freight traffic linked to the ports of Liverpool, Hull and Bristol as well as Manchester and the Pottery Towns in the Midlands.

While Cockhedge had become Warrington's second major industrial site with Peter Stub's tool factory joined by a cotton mill and glassworks, Bank Quay had also expanded. In 1815 Joseph Crosfield had begun the production of soap in a disused factory near Liverpool Road and by the 1860s Crosfield's had become one of the top five soap producers in the country. By the 1900s it had gradually expanded into a former shipyard and glassworks and fought off competition from the rival firm of William Hesketh Lever. However, in the early 1920s Sir Arthur Crosfield tired of soap manufacturing, sold the Bank Quay works to Lever Brothers of Port Sunlight.

A 1900s view of Bank Quay with Crosfield's first transporter bridge (right).

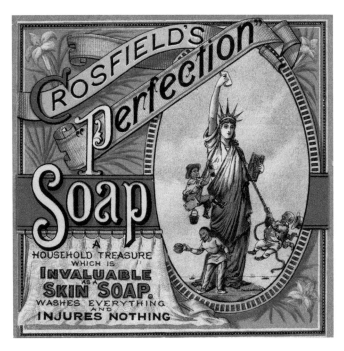

Left: An advert for one of Crosfield's popular soap brands *c.* 1900s.

Below: Whitecross wireworks contributed to the industrial pollution which hung over the town.

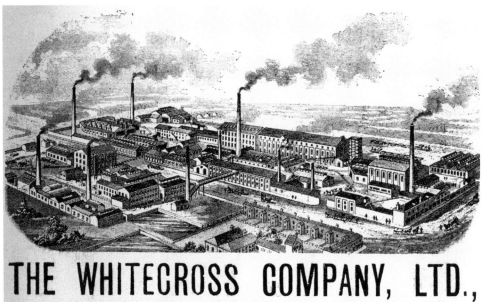

Warrington may never have been a one-industry town but by the early nineteenth century wire working was its most important trade. Firms such as Rylands, Greenings, Lockers, Whitecross and the Firth Company were major employers. The town's wire workers supplied the demands of other industries producing woven wire ropes for collieries and shipping, gauze, perforated screens, sieves and conveyor belts, together

Skilled wire-drawers at work at the
Longford Wire Iron & Steel Works.

with wire fencing and nails for builders. The 'Wire'– the original nickname of the town's rugby league club – came from the term 'Wire-pullers'.

In September 1913 a survey of *Livelihood and Poverty* demonstrated the diversity of the town's industry:

> There are in Warrington some of the largest ironworks in the United Kingdom ... also several wireworks where the processes of wire drawing and weaving are carried out. Firms manufacturing bedsteads, tubes, boilers and engines, and two of the largest gas-stove works in the country are established there... In addition there are tanneries and breweries. Other important trades are those in boxes, printing, glass, rubber, flour, white lead, timber and building materials. With so many industries upon which it is dependent, the town escapes comparatively lightly when one or a few of its trades are suffering from commercial depression or the effects of a strike.

This economic resilience helped Warrington survive the economic depression of the late 1920s to early 1930s and ensured that the town's industries played a vital role in both world wars. This diversity also helped Warrington emerge from the decline of its traditional manufacturing base in the late twentieth century and reinvent itself as a centre for business, technology and service industries thanks to its transport links.

Journalism

The year 1756 was a notable one for Warrington with the coming of its Academy and the arrival of the first newspaper to be published in Lancashire and other provincial towns. The Eyres family, who owned a printing press and bookshop, produced a few issues of *Eyres' Weekly Journal* or *The Warrington Advertiser*. Sadly the venture was not a commercial success but William Eyres Horsemarket Press developed a national reputation as printers of quality.

A century later, on 9 April 1853, Alexander Mackie launched the *Warrington Guardian* series of weekly newspapers. Inspired by the radical *Manchester Guardian*, his paper had the masthead 'Neutral in all matters Political and Religious'.

The masthead for the short-lived *Eyres Weekly Journal*.

His first editorial declared:

> To our townspeople we now commit the Warrington Guardian, trusting to their efforts, in conjunction with our own, to render the Guardian instrumental in promoting the advancement amongst us of knowledge and refinement, and earning for Warrington once more the title to the high character which it bore in former years for intellectual culture and enterprise.

By the 1870s the *Warrington Guardian* had a rival in the form of the *Warrington Examiner*, which gave a Liberal slant to the news as opposed to the *Warrington Guardian*, which was answerable to the Conservative influence of the Greenall family. Warrington's first female journalist, Mabel Capper, was appointed to the *Examiner* at the time of suffragette activity and advocated women's rights before leaving to take a leading part in the militant suffragette nationwide campaign organised by the Pankhursts.

The Warrington Examiner ceased production in 1959 but the newspaper empire begun by Mackie survived in its Warrington headquarters on Sankey Street facing the Town Hall. However, under the ownership of Eddie Shah in the 1980s it was relocated and production methods were drastically overhauled. Shah's attempts, in 1986, to make Warrington the headquarters of his new daily newspaper, *Today*, was as short-lived a venture as Eyres' *Warrington Advertiser*.

The *Warrington Guardian* has continued to chronicle the town's history under new ownership and in a traditional print issue but has a new rival in the shape of Orbit News' *Warrington Worldwide*. Both use an online edition and instant social media reporting to adapt to new global media pressures that challenge the existence of local newspapers.

Below left: Alexander Mackie, founder of the *Warrington Guardian*.

Below right: Typesetting an edition of the *Warrington Guardian* in the Sankey Street works.

Dr James Kendrick Snr and Jnr

Doctor James Kendrick Snr (1771–1847) was one of Warrington's earliest medical practitioners at a time when medicine was yet to be recognised as a profession, treatment was reserved for those who could pay and antibiotics had yet to be discovered. He resolved to provide medical care for the poor and was instrumental in founding Warrington Dispensary in 1810 to provide outpatient care for the town's poorest. Kendrick was one of two physicians, two surgeons and a dispensing chemist appointed first to a site in Orford Street and in 1819 to a house in Buttermarket Street (now adjacent to St Mary's Church).

Portrait of Dr James Kendrick Snr by Thomas Robson.

Dr James Kendrick Jnr.

However, Kendrick and his colleagues were powerless to stop an outbreak of cholera which swept through the densely occupied courtyards in the town centre in 1832 causing 112 deaths. Kendrick realised that they were hampered by lack of medical knowledge, poor sanitation and an inadequate local body to provide urgent action. He kept a record of his findings and also logged all the cases of smallpox he treated as treatment for this highly infectious disease was still in its infancy.

His son James Kendrick Jnr (1809–82) followed him into the profession after an apprenticeship at the Buttermarket Street Dispensary and graduating from Edinburgh University. He ran a successful medical practice in Warrington and as Medical Examiner for the Blue Coat School in the 1860s exposed the ill treatment suffered by the poor children in its care.

Father and son also played an important part in the town's intellectual life. Kendrick Snr was a keen botanist and zoologist and founder of Warrington Natural History Society. Kendrick Jnr was keenly interested in the town's early history and became an honorary local history curator at Warrington Museum. He organised excavations at the castle site in Church Street and Roman Wilderspool besides publishing numerous pamphlets and newspaper articles.

When the new Warrington Infirmary and Dispensary opened behind Bank Park in 1877 the street in which it stood was swiftly renamed Kendrick Street in their honour.

Latchford

The name Latchford name originated from its function as a 'ford' or crossing over a 'laecc' meaning a boggy place or stream. The thoroughfare down present-day Wash Lane marked the place where earliest travellers found the River Mersey shallow enough to be crossed on foot or by cart from the Cheshire side to Howley. Evidence of a Bronze Age settlement in the Euclid Avenue area of Grappenhall can be traced back over 4,000 years to a spot on high ground near to the ford.

In Roman times Latchford was on the fringes of the main industrial area at Wilderspool but there was a smaller settlement off Loushers Lane. The Domesday Book of 1086 made no mention of Latchford as it was regarded as part of Grappenhall.

By the mid-seventeenth century records of early Latchford households appear, including Richard Warburton's house in Wash Lane. This large half-timbered house

The Plague House and wall in Wash Lane minus the plague stone.

achieved notoriety as the Plague House, where tradition stated that several of its occupants were struck down by one of the deadly outbreaks of the contagious disease which culminated in the Great Plague of 1665. In the mid-nineteenth century human remains were found behind the house, evidently hastily buried in unconsecrated ground without even a coffin. The cornerstone of the garden wall was preserved in Warrington Museum as it was said that the occupants who were isolated inside the house crept out and left coins in a hollow which was then filled with vinegar as a disinfectant. Once the family were safely inside the neighbours would leave food and take the money. The distance to the nearest churchyard at St Wilfrid's Grappenhall probably explained the unceremonious burial.

By 1801 Latchford had begun to change dramatically. The old ford had disappeared with improvements to the navigation of the River Mersey and the Old Quay Canal which bissected the area. The area of Latchford nearest to Warrington Bridge became increasingly industrialised. In 1787 the first Boulton and Watt steam engine in the North West was installed in a Latchford cotton mill. Between 1801 and 1831 Latchford's population grew from 754 to 2,166, and the cutting of the Manchester Ship Canal in the early 1890s finally separated it from Cheshire.

Meanwhile the tanning industry had come to Latchford village, which was becoming a suburb of Warrington. The Broadbents had a tannery at Thelwall Lane and lived at

A view of the Hollies on Knutsford Road painted by Constance Broadbent.

the Hollies while the Reynolds family lived next to their tannery at Raddon Court. During the First World War Raddon Court became a Red Cross hospital run by the Broadbent sisters.

During the 1920s Warrington Borough Council began to implement new national housing legislation to provide 'homes fit for heroes' for the troops returning from the horrors of the First World War. In the 1930s Thelwall Lane, Westy and Loushers Lane all became the site of council housing estates, with the new road infrastructure of Kingsway and a second bridge over the Mersey.

Kingsway Bridge under construction.

M

The Manchester Ship Canal

Built between 1885 and 1894, this huge engineering project altered the local landscape and the old river and canal network around Warrington. New sections of waterway through Warrington were linked to the River Mersey to enable ocean-going vessels to reach the new inland port of Manchester and the neighbouring Lancashire cotton towns. Although it gave local industry another link to the ports of Liverpool and Manchester, the planned Warrington docks were not developed on the scale anticipated.

The white-shirted navvies are dwarfed by the construction work at Stockton Heath.

A large vessel leaves Latchford Lock to pass the swing bridge.

The cutting of the canal had a dramatic impact on the landscape of South Warrington. Latchford was cut off from Thelwall and Grappenhall and Wilderspool isolated from nearby Stockton Heath. Construction work on the Manchester Ship Canal in the early 1890s brought some of the first cranes and earth-moving equipment to the town, and these major new civil engineering projects brought employment opportunities for construction workers, known as navigators (or 'navvies'.) These included many Irish workers who descended en masse to the small villages like Stockton Heath along the route.

By its completion in December 1893 17,000 navvies had shifted 54 million cubic yards of soil and rocks to create the 35.5-mile-long canal at the then staggering cost of £15 million. This equated to around £2 billion in early 2019 – significantly less than similar modern infrastructure projects, because the builders of the Ship Canal could pay very low wages and have less concern about health and safety. However, they did have to provide a substitute for a traditional right of way over the redirected River Mersey by providing the so-called Penny Ferry crossing at Thelwall.

Today the greatest feats of engineering can be seen at Latchford with its parallel hydraulically operated locks, the larger of which is 183 metres long and 20 metres across. The sluice gates behind the smaller lock control the flow of water and maintain a constant level. Towering above the locks is the railway viaduct which was built to allow the tallest ships to pass beneath whilst carrying the now closed London and North Western Railway line.

The nearby Knutsford Road Bridge is one of a series of swing bridges built through the town to allow canal traffic to pass through the area's road crossings. Even though shipping on the canal had declined by the mid-twentieth century these bridges created major bottlenecks for modern-day Warrington's vastly increased volume of traffic, which the nearby Thelwall Viaduct has failed to resolve. At its construction the Manchester Ship Canal was nicknamed 'the Big Ditch' and today it effectively bisects twenty-first-century Warrington whilst bringing little commercial benefit to the town.

Museum and Library

In May 1848 Warrington Borough Council created a unique institution, the first Museum and Library to be founded under the 1845 Museum's Act. Warrington created the third oldest public museum in England and also the first in the North West. However, by using the Museum Act to have an integral library Warrington also enabled the creation of a national public library system. However, usage of the lending library was restricted to subscribers until the 1880s.

By 1853 the museum had outgrown its temporary premises in Friars Gate and thanks to the generosity of local landowner Mr Wilson Patten a new site was found off Bold Street. Plans for an ambitious building were commissioned from leading architect John Dobson, and then rejected because of their cost.

The original site of Warrington Museum and Library on the corner of Friar's Gate.

Museum & School of Art. Warrington, Lancashire.

Warrington Museum and School of Art in 1864.

A more affordable option from Mr Stone of Newton le Willows was accepted and work began on creating a 'Home for the Muses', to make art, literature and science accessible to all. The three-storey building would include galleries, reading room, library and space for the School of Art. The foundation stone was laid on 22 September 1855 by William Beamont and the building opened in December 1857.

As well as the museum galleries and a reference library the building was also the first home of Warrington's School of Art, which was organised by the Mechanics' Institute to provide an education that would allow young artists to find employment in industry. The school flourished under Christmas Thompson and produced artists of the calibre of Luke Fildes, who became an established graphic artist, illustrating *The Mystery of Edwin Drood,* Charles Dickens's last work.

Fair Quiet and Sweet Rest (now on show in the museum) helped establish Fildes' reputation when it was exhibited in the all-important Royal Academy Summer Exhibition of 1872. This idyllic scene was based on a picnic and boat trip along the Thames by Fildes and his friend, the Warrington artist Henry Woods, accompanied by Woods' two sisters. Fildes sits centre stage with a lute, serenading the seated figure of titian-haired Fanny Woods – his future wife. Henry Woods also became a successful artist whilst

Fair Quiet and Sweet Rest by Luke Fildes.

Annie married John James Webster, the architect of Warrington Bridge. Fildes became a leading member of the London arts scene, a member of the Royal Academy and was commissioned to paint the coronation portraits of Edward VII and George V.

Between 1873 and 1874 plans were drawn up for an extension along Museum Street. On the ground floor was more space for the Central Library and upstairs a new art gallery, which was officially opened on 4 October 1877 by the mayor, Samuel Mather Webster, a leading supporter of the School of Art, which relocated to a new Museum Street site in 1883.

By the 1930s the museum and library were separate entities sharing one building. A magnificent new domed lending library with art deco influences was created on the ground floor and additional museum galleries above. Despite further remodelling in the 1960s the museum has retained its distinctive character by sensitively adapting its Victorian galleries whilst a network of libraries has been created across the town. Works by Fildes and other major artists can be seen in the exhibition galleries whilst the Archives and Local Studies collection are a major resource for local historians.

Today the Museum and Central Library's resources provide an A–Z of Warrington's cultural heritage and links to our contemporary global society.

New Town

Early twenty-first-century Warrington was shaped by its designation as a New Town in 1968 and subsequent local government boundary changes of 1974. New Town status was granted to help resolve national and local pressures to deal with an expected population growth by the end of the century and its impact on the national transport infrastructure. Almost one million extra jobs and houses were needed in the North West alone and without planned development Liverpool and Manchester might have sprawled into one mass conurbation. Runcorn and Skelmersdale had already been created as New Towns and now the historic area of Warrington was to be extended. Warrington's transport links gave it the potential to become a major regional growth centre with new retail, business and industrial hubs and a new local road network linked to the national motorway system.

The creation of the New Town was also intended to solve Warrington's own planning problems by redeveloping the redundant Second World War sites of Risley munitions works and the former military bases at Burtonwood and Padgate. This was to be achieved by a Master Plan for the town whose population was expected to

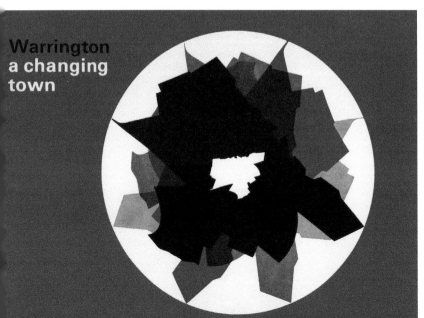

Promotional booklet for Warrington New Town sent to local households.

Part of the disused Risley Munitions site to be redeveloped for Birchwood.

rise from 65,000 in 1965 to over 200,000 by the end of the century. Work began in earnest in 1970 with implementation the responsibility of the Warrington New Town Development Corporation, set up in March 1969.

The pattern of development was to be based upon the creation of new neighbourhoods and districts, focussing on district centres providing a wide range of facilities and services. The new residential and industrial areas were to be threaded together by a comprehensive network of new roads, woven within the existing framework of the M6, M56 and M62, and including urban motorways. Crucial to the plan's success was the town's connectivity with the new motorway network, its continued railway and Ship Canal freight links and latterly two regional airports. New business parks were connected to the regional and national transport infrastructure by a series of urban motorways.

Midway through the implementation of the plan Warrington saw many of its traditional industries disappear as a result of new cheaper foreign competition and changing working practices. Although Warrington has been judged to be one of the most successful New Towns, the New Town Development Corporation was dissolved prematurely on 30 September 1989 and the responsibility for Warrington's twenty-first-century economic development ultimately devolved to the council.

Oliver Cromwell

Oliver Cromwell was a key Parliamentary general who defeated King Charles I's Royalist armies during the English Civil Wars of the 1640s. So why is his statue in Warrington?

In August 1648 Cromwell led the Parliamentary army which was trying to stop Charles I regaining the throne with Scottish support. On 19 August the two armies clashed at the Battle of Red Bank near Winwick. The Scots retreated to Warrington,

Below left: Portrait of Cromwell prior to his Irish campaign by Robert Walker.

Below right: Cromwell's statue at Bridge Foot facing the River Mersey.

where they lost a skirmish with Cromwell's troops at Warrington Bridge. Cromwell stayed the night at an inn in Church Street whilst many of his prisoners were held at what was later known as Scotland Road.

Early the following year Cromwell was one of the first to sign the king's death warrant and as a leading Parliamentarian was rewarded with an official portrait by Robert Walker which showed him in armour with his commander's baton, ready to set sail for Ireland to subdue the Irish Catholics who supported the Royalist cause. In September of 1649 Cromwell put to death the 2,500-strong garrison at Drogheda and earned the everlasting hatred of the Irish and Catholics. By 1653 Cromwell had become king in all but name with the title of Lord Protector and ruled until his death in 1658.

In 1899, 300 years after Cromwell's birth, local ironmaster Frederick Monks, who shared Cromwell's nonconformist religious beliefs, gave a statue of Cromwell by John Bell to the town. It was placed outside the original Warrington Academy at Bridge Foot, facing into Bridge Street but later relocated to face Warrington Bridge. However, Monk's gift was not welcomed by many Warringtonians of Irish descent. Moreover, it would give organisers of future royal visits to the town a major logistical problem in ensuring that the route would never pass the statue because of Cromwell's key role in the execution of a monarch.

Orford

Today it is hard to imagine that Orford was once a small country hamlet largely detached from Warrington but close to Winwick. Few areas of Warrington have been so dramatically transformed, but few have such a rich history ... which includes pineapples and a famous fashion designer!

William Yates's map of Lancashire in 1786 shows Orford in a rural landscape with Long Lane and Sandy Lane as boundaries of Orford Hall, the residence of John Blackburne Esquire. Present-day Battersby Lane provides a grand southern approach to the hall, which was home to the Blackburne family. They had lived at Orford since the early seventeenth century and were among the most prominent landowners and political figures as Lords of the Manor of Warrington. The hall itself had been largely rebuilt c. 1716 while John Blackburne (1693–1786) created its magnificent park lands.

The Blackburne family had prospered by their indirect involvement in the notorious slave trade with John Blackburne's son investing in Salt House Dock at Liverpool, a major port for slavery. The family also traded in salt, which was an important currency for buying African slaves for the West Indian plantations. Blackburne's nephew, Thomas Patten, also prospered from his copper trade with Africa and the West Indies. Blackburne's wealth and family trading connections gave him the resources to import rare plants to Orford Hall and establish his reputation as an early botanist, bringing a rare Cedar of Lebanon to his park.

ORFORD HALL.

Orford Hall in the eighteenth century.

Blackburne is probably best known for his 'pine stove', which was the first in the north of England to produce ripe pineapples. In 2001 Warrington Museum purchased a painting of John Blackburne that appears to show that he had once been holding a pineapple on his outstretched hand but this was overpainted to show the outline of the first hothouse in the north-west of England.

As Warrington became an increasingly built-up industrial town the family sold up their rights as Lords of the Manor and leased out the hall, and by 1871 Warrington's first mayor, William Beamont, was in residence. The coming of the Cheshire Lines railway in 1873 made the hall and its grounds a less tranquil environment and it faced an uncertain future.

Arthur Bennett eventually persuaded the council to buy the hall from the Blackburne family as a memorial to the lads of Warrington in the First World War. At the opening ceremony in August 1917 the mayor, Peter Peacock, promised that,

> After the war the council will formulate a scheme for the use of the hall and grounds. In the meantime the grounds will be open to the public for rest and recreation ... and the old and young people will spend many happy hours in this quiet and pleasant place. The fields behind the hall have already been thrown open as a playground for the children and I imagine the place one day laid out with bowling greens and permanent allotments. The large pond in the rear (part of the old duck decoy) will be an endless attraction to the children and when it is made safe for their use will be a fine place for paddling and for catching stickle backs.

In the post-war austerity, and without Bennett's championship, the hall decayed and was eventually demolished in the mid-1930s, although the park survived. By then Orford was becoming increasingly urbanised with a mixture of private and local authority housing and new road systems and no longer separate from Warrington. One of its post-war residents, Ossie Clark, would help keep the district on the map.

Above: The Cedar of Lebanon at Orford Hall before the hurricane of 1868.

Right: Portrait of John Blackburn by Hamlet Winstanley.

Ossie Clark

It was a dramatic arrival onto the scene for future fashion sensation Ossie, who was born during a Second World War German air raid on Walton Hospital, Liverpool. His parents, Ann and Samuel Clark, promptly christened their first son Raymond and wisely decided to evacuate the new baby and his three older sisters, Gladys, Kay and Beryl, to the relative safety of Oswaldtwistle, Lancashire. Here the family endured wartime austerity, with food and clothing rationing, relieved by Mother's home dressmaking.

In 1949 seven-year-old Raymond and his family moved to No. 5 Sandy Lane West in Orford. His new classmates at St Margaret's School promptly christened him 'Ossie' because of his broad Oswaldtwistle accent and the nickname was to stay with him for life.

The post-war Warrington of his childhood seemed a typically drab Northern town. Yet the presence of the Yanks from Burtonwood brought a glimpse of transatlantic culture – 'American cars with fins and suicide blondes', as Ossie later recalled.

In the 1950s teenager Ossie watched the local Teddy Boys 'lounging in pink day-glow socks' at the Rodney Street Boys' Club and plotted his escape. Not for him

Illustration from Warrington Museum's retrospective Ossie Clark exhibition, 1999–2000.

the 'proper jobs' awaiting an eleven-plus failure and he found an ally in his art tutor, Roy Thomas, at Beamont Technical School. Saturday morning classes at Warrington School of Art helped him secure a place at Art College in Manchester at the age of sixteen, the first stage to a career in the glamorous world of fashion, which beckoned him away from Warrington.

Ossie quickly became a key figure in the London fashion scene of the Swinging Sixties, beginning in 1964 at the stylish Chelsea boutique of Quorum. He was a master garment cutter, enhancing all who wore his designs, which were also sensuous and flamboyant. His style ranged from cool chic to the outrageously theatrical, like the jumpsuit created for Mick Jagger. Clark's skilfully cut designs were combined with the fantasy chiffon prints produced by his wife and business partner, Celia Birtwell, who he had met at art college. The translucent floating garments designed by Clark and Birtwell suited the mood of the hippies of the flower power generation. Leading fashion critic Susie Menkes later commented, 'Ossie formed the bridge between the 60's and 70's. Ossie Clark Designs were not only quintessentially of their time but led fashion forward.'

Although Ossie retained close ties with his Warrington roots and family, he relished the limelight and the excesses that high life and celebrity status could offer in London, Paris and New York. His clothes were paraded by top models Bianca Jagger, Patti Boyd Jerry Hall and Marie Helvin and photographed by David Bailey. Clark considered himself an artist and socialised with Andy Warhol, Picasso, Salvador Dali and his lifelong friend from college days David Hockney.

After the end of his marriage and business partnership with Celia in 1974 his erratic lifestyle saw his fashion output wane. The punk era of the 1980s and lack of business acumen led to bankruptcy before a partial revival cut short by his premature death in 1996.

Padgate

Padgate derives its name from the Old English words for a path (pad) and a way (gate) – since the district sat on an ancient route from Warrington to Bolton via Leigh. Padgate was part of Poulton with Fearnhead with the latter place name meaning an area of high ground covered with ferns. Until 1873 the whole area was largely agricultural with a few scattered farms until the coming of the railway station on the new Cheshire Line between Liverpool and Manchester saw a small settlement develop near the station.

From 1939 to 1957 the population of Padgate was swelled by thousands of Royal Air Force (RAF) recruits. Number 3 RAF Depot Padgate opened in April 1939 as part of Britain's preparation for a second world war. The War Office requisitioned over 300 acres of farmland from Blackbrook to Padgate and Houghton Green and within a month the training centre, accommodation huts, and parade grounds appeared on a site which often flooded.

Distinguished First World War pilot Group Captain Gilbert Insall VC was the first camp commander responsible for instilling basic discipline into raw young recruits, kitting them out with uniform and military haircuts and assessing their permanent service roles.

The entrance to Number 3 RAF Depot Padgate Camp.

As the war progressed RAF Padgate's intake increased to 7,000 to meet the turnover of bombing crews attacking enemy territory. Local residents became familiar with the sounds of military exercises and machine-gun fire while Padgate's churches provided welcome social events and a surrogate family atmosphere for homesick youths.

After the war ended in 1945 Padgate camp continued to give eight weeks' basic training for young men undertaking their National Service in the RAF, including future Rolling Stone Bill Wyman. Group Captain Insall returned for the final passing out ceremony in 1957.

The site fell into disuse until the 1980s when it was redeveloped as part of Warrington New Town plans. Links to the former camp were retained with streets named after former RAF aircraft such as the Wellington bomber and the road at the heart of the old site named Insall Road.

National Service recruits at Padgate in the 1950s.

Group Captain Insall takes the salute at Padgate.

Queen and Country

During the reign of Queen Victoria (1837–1901) Britain saw itself as a major world power and had ambitions to extend its empire. Many Warrington men felt it was their patriotic duty to fight for 'Queen and Country' in the armed forces, even though many had never left their home town before.

During the Crimean War of 1854–56 Britain and France fought on the side of the Turkish Empire in its struggle with Russia for control of the Black Sea and the Crimea peninsula. Over 400 Warrington soldiers enlisted as humble foot soldiers or joined

Below left: Private Thomas Wright (left) and Sergeant James Nunnerley (centre) with campaign medals.

Below right: A contemporary illustration of the Charge of the Light Brigade.

the more dashing cavalry regiments, including Private Thomas Wright and Sergeant James Nunnerley, who were at the heart of the action serving with the 17th Lancers.

On 25 October 1854 they were part of the infamous Charge of the Light Brigade at the Battle of Balaclava, which was being defended by British, French and Turkish Troops. British commander Lord Raglan ordered Lord Lucan to lead a cavalry attack to capture Russian guns. Warrington's Sergeant James Donoghue of the 8th Hussars sounded the bugle call to advance. In the confusion the Light Cavalry brigade were mistakenly directed into an attack by Russian guns and around 22,000 men.

This cavalry charge ended in one of the bloodiest defeats in British military history but the survivors became folk heroes. In the carnage of a battle lasting barely half an hour 113 men and 475 horses were killed with 247 men badly wounded. Miraculously Donoghue survived, although his horse was shot from under him. Wright and Nunnerley went on to fight at Inkermann and the Siege of Sebastopol where Warrington's Private William Norman was awarded the Victoria Cross for his actions in battle.

Victoria's portrait on the Queen's Gardens drinking fountain.

In April 1858 two cannons captured at Sebastopol were presented to Warrington and placed outside the newly built Arpley Station near Bridge Foot. Nunnerley went on to serve with the Lancashire Hussars, becoming a Sergeant Major. Donoghue lived in retirement at Penketh and gave talks on his Crimean experiences whilst Wright fell on hard times and had to pawn his war medals to survive. The Arpley cannons were removed on 22 June 1940 and recycled for the scrap metal drive to build military equipment for the Second World War. The commemorative plaques were salvaged and later placed in Queen's Gardens, which has close associations with another major campaign of Queen Victoria's reign.

In 1897 Queen Victoria celebrated sixty years on the throne and Warrington's town council decided to mark her Diamond Jubilee by providing a public park at the heart of the town centre. After the private gardens in the centre of Palmyra Square were bought in March 1897 Robert Garnett, a wealthy local businessman, presented a suitable royal centrepiece: a cast-iron drinking fountain manufactured by MacFarlane's Glasgow Foundry and bearing a portrait of the queen herself.

When Warrington wanted to honour members of the South Lancashire regiment killed in the Boer War what better place to site the memorial than in gardens dedicated to the queen? In 1889 war had broken out between Britain and the Boer republic in South Africa when the forces of President Kruger of the Transvaal attacked the neighbouring British territory in Cape Colony and Natal. They besieged British garrisons at Ladysmith, Mafeking and Kimberley. Troops were sent out from

Lieutenant Colonel O'Leary.

Memorial to O'Leary and Warrington's Boer War soldiers in Queen's Gardens.

Britain led by General Sir Redvers Buller and hundreds of men from Warrington and the surrounding area joined the South Lancashire Volunteers. In February 1900 the regiment was involved in heavy fighting to relieve the town of Ladysmith and Lieutenant Colonel McCarthy O'Leary was killed in action at a battle at Pieters Hill.

In February 1907 an expectant crowd arrived in Queen's Gardens to witness General Sir Redvers Buller unveil the memorial on a day when 'the sun shone brightly and banners and streamers flew in the breeze'. After a civic reception at the Town Hall the ceremony began at 3 p.m. Sculptor Alfred Drury invited the distinguished war hero to unveil the bronze statue which 'represented the late Colonel McCarthy O'Leary as he appeared in the Battle of Pieters Hill where he fell directing his troops'. Commemorative plaques also record all the men of the regiment killed in the South African campaign and a list of the engagements they fought. Each February Queen's Gardens is the focus of a military ceremony to remember these gallant soldiers whilst Warringtonians killed in later conflicts are remembered at the Cenotaph at Bridge Foot each November.

River Mersey

The name Mersey means 'Boundary River' and through history Warrington's river has separated successive administrative districts. In Roman times it was the boundary between warring Celtic tribes and in the ninth century it separated the Anglo-Saxon kingdom of Mercia and Viking Northumbria. The Anglo-Saxon Chronicle records that in AD 923 Edward King of Mercia visited Thelwall and ordered the strengthening of the fortification there (known as a burh) as defence against Viking attacks. However, since the course of the Mersey has changed considerably over the centuries the actual site could actually have been on Thelwall Eye, later part of Latchford.

By medieval times the ford at Warrington had become a major node on the emerging regional road system. This crossing was controlled by the Boydell family of Grappenhall but by at least 1280 this had been supplanted by the initial wooden bridge built by the Boteler family. When this bridge collapsed in the early 1450s travellers were left to cross by ford and ferry again. In 1495 King Henry VII opened the first substantial three-arched stone bridge provided by the Earl of Derby.

Fishing scene at Latchford in the 1790s with the parish church on the right.

By the early eighteenth century the Mersey between Warrington and Liverpool had been made navigable for river traffic to reach the emerging port at Bank Quay and stimulate the town's growing industries. Baines Directory of 1825 recorded that,

> At the time of the spring tides, the Mersey rises from ten to twelve feet at Warrington Bridge and vessels from 70 to 100 tons burden can navigate the river to this point. The communication between Manchester and Liverpool, by means of this navigation is incessant.

Warrington's fishing industry also thrived; an engraving of the River Mersey from Knutsford Road in the 1790s shows men netting shoals of sparlings. The Universal Directory of 1792 recorded that, 'In the river are caught sturgeons, greenbacks, mullets, sand eels, lobsters, shrimps, prawns, and the best and largest cockles in all of England.'

Overfishing and the growth of industry along the riverbanks had killed off the trade within another fifty years and also Warrington's short-lived annual midsummer regatta which took place from the 1840s between Fiddler's Ferry and Warrington Bridge.

Warrington Regatta competitions in progress in the early 1840s.

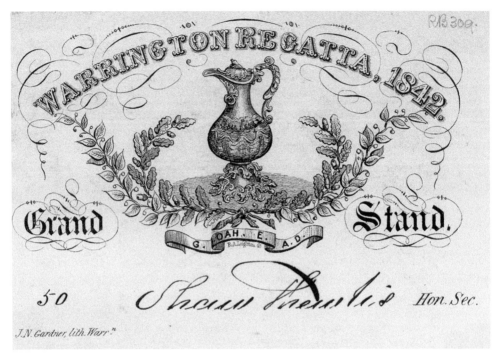

Grand stand ticket for the Regatta festival at Arpley in 1842.

An 1897 view of the three-arched Victoria Bridge looking towards Howley.

A variety of craft competed for trophies including the Borough Cup of silver oars. Field games and gambling on the outcome of the races took place on Arpley Meadows, culminating in a wheelbarrow race and oatcake eating contest! In 1863 a former competitor noted that 'the river became so much polluted that it was no longer a pleasure to row on it'.

By the end of the century many of Warrington's major industries used the Mersey to transport goods to Bank Quay and Bishops Wharf near Bridge Foot but the Victoria Bridge, which had opened in 1837, was proving a barrier to river transport whilst it was already clear that this narrow bridge could not cope with the growing volume of road traffic: 'There is not a single improvement in Warrington which is more urgently needed ... and everybody has been crying out for a new bridge for years,' declared Councillor Arthur Bennett, who had masterminded the project.

In 1911 work finally began on the construction of a new reinforced-concrete bridge designed by Warrington-born J. J. Webster. The first half was opened on 7 July 1913 by King George V and in April 1915 the new bridge was revealed in all its glory in the midst of the First World War. Webster's bridge also proved inadequate. Despite the construction of the motorways bypassing the town and the construction of a second river crossing at Bridge Foot in the 1990s, Warrington's Mersey crossing remains a traffic bottleneck until additional bridging points are created for twenty-first-century traffic demands.

Webster's Bridge, opened in 1915, and remnant of the Victoria Bridge.

Sporting Heroes

For many Warringtonians the focus of the town's sporting glory is Warrington Wolves' rugby league stadium. Formed in 1876, Warrington's club became one of the founders of the Northern Rugby Football Union in 1895 and helped make the breakaway from rugby union to rugby league football. Until the advent of the Super League in 1996 the team were known as 'The Wire' – a nickname derived from the 'wire-pullers', who were the elite workers in Warrington's major wire industry.

In 2004 the club officially vacated its historic Wilderspool stadium for a new ground on Winwick Road adjacent to the Tesco superstore. Two monuments to Brian Bevan,

Tributes to rugby league legend Brian Bevan at Warrington Wolves' Stadium.

Warrington's legendary Australian winger (1948–62) are a prominent reminder of the club's heritage at the stadium entrance. The statue of Bevan in action was relocated from its original Wilderspool site whilst a new portrait of inscribed bricks in the club's famous blue and yellow colours was installed nearby. The club's history is well-documented on its heritage wall inside the stadium but other Warrington sporting heroes also deserve mention, not least a legendary flat-racing jockey.

Steve Donoghue was born in Warrington in November 1884 and by the age of twelve was working in a local steelworks. He decided to become a jockey after winning a donkey race at a circus. After serving his apprenticeship and becoming a stable jockey he had his first major success in 1913. Between 1914 and 1923 he was champion jockey for ten consecutive years, winning 946 races in that period. His other major feat was to win the Derby on six occasions (in 1915, 1917, 1921, 1922, 1923 and 1925).

In 1915 and 1917 Donoghue won the Triple Crown of the Three Thousand Guineas, the Derby and St Leger Stakes. He was the only jockey to have won it twice in its 2,000-year history. He won the last of over 2,000 races in 1932 and retired from racing at the age of fifty-two. Racing success did not translate into sustained financial wealth. He died of a heart attack on 23 March 1945.

Other past local sporting heroes competing for mention must include George Duckworth, Lancashire and England test cricketer (1901–66); Ethel 'Sunny' Lowry, the first British woman to swim the English Channel; and Culcheth-born Roger Hunt, a member of England's 1966 World Cup-winning team.

Steve Donoghue by John A. A. Berrie,
R. A. (Warrington Museum)

Tragedy at Sea

The tragedy of the White Star Line's Titanic is widely known but Warrington's association through the *Tayleur* and E. J. Smith deserves greater recognition.

In the mid-1850s, Warrington made a short-lived bid to be considered as a shipbuilding town from Tayleur & Sanderson's Bank Quay yard. In 1853 they launched the *Tayleur*, the largest iron ship yet constructed on the Mersey. The construction of the ship had only taken six months and the equally newly launched *Warrington Guardian* reported that 'She is double-riveted throughout, and will be the strongest built craft afloat, being divided into five water-tight compartments. The total quantity of iron about her is 780 tons.'

It seemed that the whole of Warrington turned out to see the launch of the *Tayleur* on 4 October 1853. The omens seemed good as she floated swiftly and gracefully into the Mersey to be towed to Liverpool to be rigged and fitted for her voyage to Australia.

The *Tayleur* in full sail before the disaster of her maiden voyage.

On 19 January 1854 the *Tayleur* set sail for Melbourne crowded with 660 emigrants eager to seek their fortunes in Australia. On 23 January the stunned inhabitants of Warrington heard that the ship had run aground off Lambay Island in Dublin Bay two days earlier during a storm, just two days into her epic voyage. The magnificent ship was a wreck and around 426 of the 660 passengers and crew had died.

The survivors had harrowing tales to tell:

Wives clinging to their husbands, children to their parents .... Great numbers of women jumped overboard but three women only out of 200 were saved... The ship's stern now began to sink ... every wave washed off scores at a time; we could see them struggling for a moment, then, tossing their arms, sink to rise no more. At length the whole of the ship sank under water... From the time the ship first struck, till she went down was not more than twenty minutes.

At the ensuing coroner's inquest the owners were held largely to blame for a number of errors including failing to realise that the *Tayleur*'s iron hull would cause misleading compass readings that would take the ship aground.

Sixty years later in an uncanny echo of the *Tayleur* tragedy, the White Star Line lost another apparently unsinkable ship on its maiden voyage carrying emigrants to a new world. When RMS *Titanic* left Southampton bound for America on 10 April 1912 well-respected Captain Edward John Smith was at its helm. Smith was born in the Potteries but later operated from the port of Liverpool. He was one of the White Star Line's most experienced captains and the company's fortune was largely riding on the success of the voyage. However, four days out of Southampton, at 11.40 p.m., the *Titanic* struck an iceberg in the North Atlantic and sank less than three hours later with the loss of 1,500 lives including its captain. The *Titanic*'s story made headline news across the world but had a special resonance in Warrington because the captain's widow was Winwick-born Sarah Eleanor Pennington, whom he had married at St Oswald's Church in 1887.

The Thames Board Mills Bombing

The Thames Board incident of 14 September 1940 was Warrington's worst atrocity during the Second World War. Despite the number of military bases and crucial war industries around the town Warrington escaped a serious blitz. It was clear from German aerial photographs that the Luftwaffe (German air force) was aware of crucial targets, including the nearby Manchester Ship Canal. Perhaps the dense fog which often hid the town was the town's saviour, or more likely neighbouring Liverpool and Manchester were considered greater priorities.

All this changed one fine Saturday afternoon in early autumn as families were enjoying a fete on Thames Board Mill's recreation ground in Arpley Meadows.

A contemporary police photograph showing the devastation of the Thames Board incident.

The events were vividly recorded in the local papers, portraying the incident as a wartime atrocity. They expressed the outrage felt by the whole town but were careful not to name the actual site, to avoid letting the enemy know the outcome of the attack. 'Bomber Kills Women, Babies', screamed one headline:

> Mothers and tiny babies were among the helpless civilians killed by a lone German raider who swooped down upon them in a North-West town. They were attending a Spitfire gala in a recreation club when the bomber dived without warning and released two bombs. One completely wrecked the light wooden club … two families were partly wiped out, members of others lie in hospital gravely wounded. It was all over in seconds … but dead, dying, injured and a mass of mangled debris were the pitiful aftermath which this Nazi bomber left behind as, immediately he swept back into the skies and vanished.

Later there were many conflicting eyewitness accounts from those who had seen the plane swoop over the town, but most agreed that the pilot was low enough to see exactly what he had bombed. The Warrington Fire Officer's log reported, however, that German radio reports that evening claimed that the nearby Aluminium Mills at Bank Quay had been bombed.

The sixteen innocent victims and many more casualties were finally remembered in September 1991 with the unveiling of a simple commemorative plaque on the former Thames Board site, now known as Centre Park.

U

USAAF Burtonwood

During the Second World War Warrington was the site of several key military bases and saw a friendly invasion of Americans stationed at Burtonwood airbase. RAF Burtonwood had opened in 1939, just in time for the crucial Battle of Britain, and the United States Army Air Force, which took over in 1942, played a vital support role for the war in Europe.

A ceremonial presentation of the American flag at Warrington Town Hall.

Burtonwood engine test beds preparing USAAF aircraft for active service.

Remote from Luftwaffe bases but close to the port of Liverpool, technicians of the USAAF assembled and maintained over 15,000 aircraft, including every B17 *Flying Fortress*, the 8th American Army Air Force's main bomber, which flew in the Second World War. Over 15,000 aircraft spent time at Burtonwood, including the famous *Memphis Belle*, but no aircraft ever took off from Burtonwood to attack enemy targets. The base became the largest military installation in Europe, larger than Heathrow today.

Burtonwood USAAF Airbase had a great impact on the town. The American GIs became a familiar sight about the town whilst the noise of engines from the test beds was heard day and night. The Yanks brought music, glamour and a foreign culture of baseball, burgers and soda fountains. Hollywood glamour came too with Bing Crosby, Bob Hope, and James Cagney boosting morale, while the legendary Glen Miller gave his last live performance at the base. The GIs spent their dollars in Warrington's pubs, cinemas and dance halls and flirted with local girls. Many became GI brides and crossed the Atlantic to form a lasting bond between the American 'invaders' and their Warrington hosts.

Burtonwood airbase also played a vital role in the Berlin Air Lift of 1948 and through the era of the Cold War. Between 1948 and 1958 the base expanded to cover

Local children are presented with scarce wartime Christmas gifts at Burtonwood.

Many local
women became
GI brides or found
employment at
Burtonwood base.

a 15-mile site. After the Berlin Air Lift Burtonwood's purpose again was to support the USAF's 14,000 British operations. The base and its occupants also had a major economic impact, spending millions of dollars with local businesses and employing thousands of local civilians.

In 1967 Burtonwood became the largest US base in Europe as a US Army General Depot and the base's mile-long Header House warehouse stored everything the US Army might need in the event of war in Europe. During Operation Desert Storm in the Gulf War and the parallel conflict in Yugoslavia in the early 1990s it was rumoured that the supply depot held everything from a safety pin to a Sherman tank.

Apart from the area occupied by the US Army much of Burtonwood base fell into decline from the mid-1960s. In 1965 plans for a Burtonwood International airport failed to get off the ground when the Ministry of Aviation decided against a third regional airport there. The main runway disappeared with the construction of part of the M62 motorway along its length. In 1982 further parts of the base were handed over for the development of the Westbrook District of Warrington's New Town.

On 17 April 1988 a symbolic landmark disappeared when demolition expert Fred Dibnah felled the 'new' control tower. Once the US Army pulled out of the base in 1993 its fate was effectively sealed. Soon new districts of Callands, Westbrook, Chapelford, Gemini and Omega covered the former base.

Villains

Heroic figures may feature in Warrington's history but there is a peculiar fascination with law breakers and scoundrels, with some even achieving the status of folk heroes. Captain Thomas Blood, the son-in-law of wealthy Culcheth landowner Colonel John Holcroft, achieved such notoriety in 1671 for his brief theft of the crown jewels. This and other crimes should have seen him face a traitor's death, but King Charles II seemed charmed by his audacity and pardoned him.

However, Edward Miles was a true villain, not least for his part in an infamous robbery along Manchester Road at Woolston in 1791 which had none of the romance attached to legendary highwayman Dick Turpin.

In the early hours of Thursday 15 September 1791 twenty-four-year-old post office employee James Hogwarth rode out of Warrington carrying mail and money bound for Manchester. Near Bruche Bridge he was ambushed by an armed gang, who tied him up, stole his mailbags, beat him around the head, cut his throat and left him to drown in the brook. The incident was described in the regional press as 'a most melancholy circumstance'. Warrington was horrified by the crime, not least because Hogwarth's widow was heavily pregnant. The post office offered a substantial reward of £200 (c. £30,000 in 2019) for the robbery to prevent similar crimes against the vulnerable carriers of the Royal Mail.

The reward posters, which had conflicting descriptions of the alleged criminals, were widely circulated. There were two chief suspects: Thomas Fleming and Edward Miles, who 'was morally certain to be one of the Mail Robbers'. Both men were linked to passing banknotes known to have been in Hogwarth's mailbag and also being part of a gang counterfeiting money. Fleming was captured first, but was sentenced to death for a different highway robbery.

Miles escaped capture until 1793 when he was put on trial at Lancaster Castle and found guilty of the charge of the Woolston robbery but not of murder. Much of the evidence against him was circumstantial but his counterfeiting activities alone made him a villain who deserved the death penalty. He was hanged at Lancaster and his body was taken back to Woolston, coated in tar to preserve it and hung in chains on a wooden gibbet frame to act as a deterrent to other highway robbers. In fact, it was

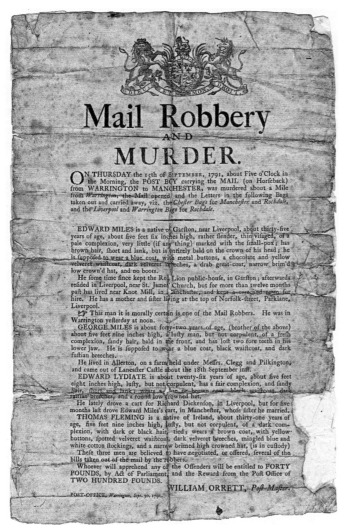

Above: The gibbet iron made to display Miles' body at the murder scene.

Left: Reward poster for Edward Miles and other alleged attackers of James Hogwarth.

the eerie noise of the gibbet swinging in the wind and the grisly sight of Miles' bones exposed by wildlife as they rode past it on a dark night that prompted the post boys to ask for its removal.

Around fifty years later the gibbet irons were taken to nearby Bruche Hall and kept in the stables until they were taken to Warrington Museum by William Beamont.

Wilderspool

Wilderspool, or 'the pool of the wild beasts' in Old English, is best known as the former location of Warrington's rugby stadium and Greenall's brewery. However, this was once a bustling centre of the Roman Empire, as exhibits from the site on show at Warrington Museum can testify. Since the cutting of the Bridgewater Canal in the 1770s, substantial evidence has been recovered to prove the existence of an important Roman settlement at Wilderspool and neighbouring Loushers Lane and Stockton Heath. Earlier historians claimed that an unidentified Roman site called *Veratinum* between Chester and Wigan explained the origins of Warrington and its name.

Established by AD 100, Wilderspool was a natural strategic site for a Roman settlement as a river crossing point. No clear evidence to support theories of a military base or port has been discovered but excavations have revealed it was an

Roman actor's mask found near St Thomas's Church at Stockton Heath.

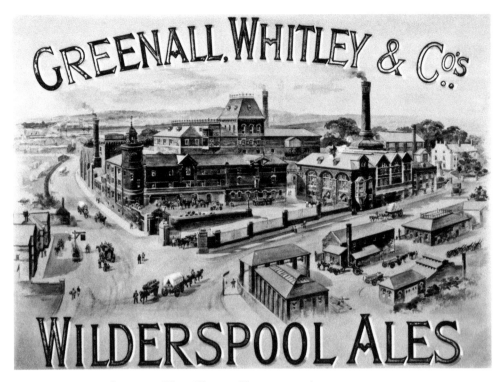

Advertising poster for Greenall's Wilderspool brewery, early 1900s.

important Romano-British industrial settlement lasting for at least two centuries. Raw materials needed to make the pottery, metalwork and glass produced in Wilderspool's workshops alongside the key Roman Road could easily be imported and its products transported to other Roman sites.

In the 1860s Dr James Kendrick (the younger) revealed important evidence of pottery making near St Thomas's Church, including a rare Roman actor's mask. Few similar masks have been found anywhere else in Roman Britain, or possibly the entire Roman Empire. It was probably intended for the theatre production at the Roman fort at Chester and later analysis revealed it was made from local clay.

Excavating during the construction of the Manchester Ship Canal between 1895 and 1904, Thomas May discovered a major industrial site near Greenall's brewery. There was evidence of furnaces for iron and bronze working, enameling and possibly glass making.

A second Roman site at Loushers Lane excavated in the 1930s revealed a large building with the remains of underfloor central heating (or hypocaust) and suggested that Wilderspool's British workforce may have been supervised by a Roman site manager. A heatwave in the 1970s uncovered the site of the Roman cemetery on the banks of the Ship Canal but it is unlikely that the full extent of Roman Wilderspool has been discovered, despite more recent exploration of the former Greenall's brewery site.

The Greenall brewing dynasty was already well established at Wilderspool by 1791, headed by St Helens brewer Thomas Greenall. Good supplies of pure well water, together with ample quantities of locally grown grain for malting, a good transport network and wealthy investors made Warrington an ideal choice for expansion. Rivals like Walker's (later Tetley Walker) and Burtonwood Ales followed but the Greenalls integrated into local public life, becoming not only major employers but also in Sir Gilbert Greenall's case the town's MP with a fine residence at Walton Hall.

By the early 1900s the Wilderspool Brewery had been completely rebuilt whilst their earlier on-site home of the White House remained as offices. The firm owned a number of licensed houses in Lancashire, Cheshire, North Wales, Shropshire, Staffordshire and other areas as well as the majority of the hotels and inns in Warrington.

From the 1960s brewing was no longer a profitable industry and pubs were losing business from competition from cheap beer on sale in supermarkets. In 1991 Greenalls ended the brewing of beer at Wilderspool after almost 250 years, and in 1999 disposed of all their public houses and restaurants. The Wilderspool brewery site is now largely a gated business park and an adjacent supermarket.

X for the Ballot Box

It was not until 1928 that all Warringtonians of voting age gained the right to put an X on the ballot paper in local and parliamentary elections. The struggle for democracy had begun in 1832 when the area then known as Warrington gained the right to return an MP to Parliament. Then only 379 people in Warrington could vote in the election of December 1832, out of an adult male population of around 7,000.

Nineteenth-century elections were fought between the Whigs (later the Liberal party) and the Conservatives. Without a secret ballot until 1872 voters often felt intimidated to vote for the major landowners or employers. From 1834 John Ireland Blackburne, the Lord of the Manor, and Gilbert Greenall, head of the brewery firm, won sweeping victories for the Conservatives at parliamentary elections. In 1868, however, the last election in Warrington before the introduction of the secret ballot

A REMINISCENCE OF THE WARRINGTON ELECTION. 1868.
"I GOT THAT VOTE; DID I NOT DESERVE IT?"

Cartoon showing Gilbert Greenall supposedly squeezing out votes in the disputed election.

Above left: Peter Rylands, Gilbert Greenall's opponent in 1868.

Above right: Constance Harvey Broadbent, Warrington's first female councillor.

caused a sensation. Gilbert Greenall, who had been returned unopposed since 1852, faced a Liberal rival in Peter Rylands from the major wire-making firm.

Greenall's majority of seventy-eight was overturned after a protest by the Liberals. Rylands was declared the victor by twenty-seven votes, and both sides claimed bribery, corruption and fraud. However, the Conservatives were victorious in successive elections until 1906, with Sir Gilbert Greenall returned again from 1874–80 and 1885–92.

With the Liberals supreme in national politics, local Liberal industrialist Arthur Crosfield represented the town from 1906 until 1910 when Conservative dominance was restored. Nationally and locally the Liberals lost ground to the newly emerging Labour party, especially when the right to vote was extended to the majority of working-class men.

In the 1918 local elections Constance Harvey Broadbent (1864–1943) stood as a Conservative candidate for Latchford ward as one of the first Warrington women to seek political office under the provisions of the 1918 Representation of the People Act. She won a sweeping victory against the Labour candidate Charles Dukes. Her triumph was not merely a result of her recognised public service but because Conservative, Liberals and women voters united against a left-wing Labour candidate who many still regarded as unpatriotic for his wartime stance as a conscientious objector.

Charles Dukes, Warrington's first Labour MP.

Dukes had moved to Warrington in 1893 and started work as a labourer in a Warrington ironworks. By 1911 he had become a full-time union secretary. He joined the Independent Labour Party in 1899 and by 1912 had moved further left, becoming a member of the board of the national executive of the newly formed British Socialist Party.

During the First World War he attracted national attention when he was imprisoned for refusing to serve either on the battlefield or in other roles open to conscientious objectors. Dukes was undaunted by his defeat in the 1918 local elections and in the general election of 1923 was returned as Warrington's first Labour MP. His parliamentary career was relatively short-lived but his trade union career flourished and by 1946 he was president of the Trade Union Congress. In 1947 he was elevated to the House of Lords as Lord Dukeston, although other Labour veterans felt this had betrayed his socialist principles.

By 1945 Warrington had become a safe Labour seat, allowing the election of the town's first woman MP, Edith Summerskill, in 1955. As Warrington's MP she campaigned to improve the town's poor air quality caused by industrial pollution. She was Parliamentary Secretary to the Ministry of Food (1945–50) and Minister of National Insurance (1950–51), a member of the Labour Party's National Executive Committee from 1944 to 1958, and served as chair of the Labour Party (1954–55). She left the House of Commons and was created a life peeress as Baroness Summerskill on 4 February 1961. Redrawing of the parliamentary boundaries in 1983 created two Warrington constituencies with Labour retaining a stronghold in local and national elections in Warrington North. Warrington South included more areas with a Conservative or Liberal tradition and has been more marginal.

Y

You'll Never Believe It! Old Billy

Warrington has a number of record-breaking facts including being the first paved town in Lancashire and the site of the country's first commercial canal when the Sankey-St Helens Canal was cut in 1755–57. However, a brown and white horse and a very large oak tree deserve special mention.

Old Billy is probably the only Warrington character to appear in a *Guinness Book of Records*. This sturdy horse was bred in 1760 by Edward Robinson of Wild Grave Farm in Woolston, near Warrington, and first worked as a plough horse on the farm.

Old Billy in retirement at the Old Warps estate at Latchford.

However, most of his working life was spent in the service of the Mersey and Irwell Navigation Company (or the Old Quay Canal Company). Old Billy was first used to walk along a canal-side path towing the flatboats against the river current. When he was too old for this work he continued to be employed until 1819 as a 'gin horse' helping to raise and lower loads from the boats by powering the hoist or 'gin' on the canal bank.

In 1819 Old Billy was retired to a farm at the Old Warps Estate at Latchford (now part of Victoria Park) where he was commemorated in a number of paintings. A final highlight of his career was to take part in the coronation parade of King George IV in Manchester in 1821. Old Billy was towed along on a cart with a garland of flowers round his neck and was affectionately received by the crowds as by then he was a well-known local character.

He died on 27 November 1822 and the Manchester Natural History Society decided that his great age made his body worthy of preservation. Sadly, all that remains today is his skull, which is on display at Manchester Museum, and his stuffed head far away in Bedford Museum. However, his reputation has fared better as he is still honoured as the longest-lived horse in the world.

The Winwick Broad Oak

The Winwick Broad Oak was a national landmark and it is said that a thousand soldiers once sheltered beneath it! It covered an area of around 100 yards (*c*. 91.5 metres) with its lowest branches around 7 feet 6 inches (4.2 metres) above the ground whilst its trunk had a diameter of 14 feet (4.2 metres) at the base. Its enormous size and position near to St Oswald's Church made it an ideal site for a local celebration in 1811. The villagers held a dinner party for 124 people beneath its canopy in an event which a contemporary claimed was 'never exceeded in respectability upon any of the public occasion in Lancashire'.

The dinner was to celebrate a naval victory against the French at Lissa by Captain Phipps Hornby during the Napoleonic Wars. The scale of Hornby's achievement seemed to merit this local event, not least because he was the third son of the rector of Winwick and the Hornby family were connected by marriage to the Earl of Derby, one of the most powerful figures in the region.

The banquet tables were arranged in a semicircle around the trunk whilst the inside of the canopy was decked with white cloth to give it the appearance of a tent. There were loyal toasts and celebratory songs, one of which seemed strangely prophetic of the fates of both the tree and Hornby:

Renowned for generous shade, behold in me,
A monarch oak of thrice a century...
Since I must yield to time's relentless way,

Contemporary print of the 1811 banquet under the Winwick Broad Oak.

Resign my bark and cast my leaves away;
While Hornby's name unhurt by chance or fate.
Unchanging still, shall be for ever great.

On 4 February 1850 the Winwick Broad Oak was felled in a great gale but by then Phipps Hornby had risen to the rank of rear admiral.

Zoology and Natural History

Zoology, or the study of the animal kingdom, is just one branch of natural history where Warrington figures have established a reputation outside their native town.

Anna Blackburne (1726–93), the youngest daughter of noted botanist John Blackburne of Orford Hall, developed her own museum of natural history. She corresponded with eminent Swedish natural scientist Carl Linnaeus, who named a variety of an American bird after her called the *Sylvia Blackburniae*. After her father's death, she moved to Fairfield, a new house opposite St Elphin's Church, where a room was set aside for her collection. She was so well respected that she was included in a national 'Obituary of Considerable Persons; with Biographical Anecdotes' in the *Gentleman's Magazine* of February 1794.

Silhouette portrait of Anna Blackburne (1726–93).

Philip Pearsall Carpenter, honorary curator
at Warrington Museum.

In 1848 one of the origins of Warrington Museum was the collections of Warrington
Natural History Society. **William Wilson** (1799–1871), its president, corresponded
with fellow botanist John Stephen Henslow, who was working on a project on the
nature of species. This was developed by his pupil Charles Darwin in his work *On the
Origin of Species*. Henslow introduced Wilson to William James Hooker, who would
become director of the Royal Botanic Gardens at Kew. Wilson subsequently produced
a major work on British mosses called *Bryologica Britannica* and was also a major
donor of British plants and mosses to Warrington Museum and the national Natural
History Museum, also founded in 1848.

Meanwhile **Philip Pearsall Carpenter** (1819–77) combined his ministry of Cairo
Street Chapel with a passion for conchology (collecting and studying mollusc shells).
He became the Honorary Curator of Molluscs at Warrington Museum in 1848. In
1855 he bought the Reigen Mazatlan collection, one of the greatest shell collections in
Europe, comprising around 14 tons. He donated over 8,000 specimens to the British
Museum in 1857, but kept many others for study. On a tour of America in 1859–60 he
was asked by the Smithsonian Institution of Washington to help catalogue their shell
collection. The Smithsonian's Annual Report from 1860 states:

We have employed a distinguished conchologist, Mr. P. P. Carpenter of Warrington,
England to classify and label the extensive collection of shells, and have been
favoured in this work with the co-operation of the principal gentleman most
distinguished in this country for their original investigations in this branch of
natural history.

Above: Warrington Museum
Bird Room in 1907 laid out on
evolutionary lines by Greening.

Left: A page from Linnaeus
Greening's Nature Notebooks.

Meanwhile **Thomas Glazebrook Rylands** and **Linnaeus Greening**, from two of Warrington's major wire-making firms, devoted themselves to studying natural history at a time when their business activities were helping to destroy the town's ecology. While Rylands donated his collection of rocks and minerals to the museum, Greenings concentrated on birds, reptiles, amphibians and spiders and developed the displays on evolutionary lines, inspired by a personal meeting with Darwin. Greening also produced meticulous nature notebooks which remain an invaluable record for the museum of Warrington's early twentieth-century natural habitats.

In 1908 the museum acquired one of its most popular natural history exhibits in the shape of a large grey seal that had probably swum up the Mersey in search of salmon and became trapped at Paddington Lock. Rather than mount a rescue operation to take it back to deeper waters it was shot and eventually bought by the museum, attracting 14,000 visitors who were amazed by its sheer size.

Today seals and salmon have returned to the Mersey at Warrington, although the town's parks and greenbelt land are increasingly under threat from urban sprawl. Hopefully enough will survive to inspire a new generation of local naturalists and zoologists to preserve the town's habitats from the growing threats to the world's ecology.

The grey seal trapped in Paddington Lock is prepared for display in 1908.

Bibliography

Beamont, William, *Annals of the Lords of Warrington* (1873)

Beamont, William, *Walks About Warrington* (1887) (and other publications on Orford, Latchford etc.)

Crosby, Alan, *A History of Warrington* (Phillimore & Co. Ltd, 2002)

Crosby, Alan and Janice Hayes, *Warrington For Ever* (Wharncliffe Books, 2006)

Carter, G. A., Warrington and the Mid Mersey Valley (1971)

Carter, G. A. with J. P. Aspden, *Warrington Hundred* (1947)

Hayes, Janice, *Warrington at Work* (Stroud: Amberley Publishing, 2017)

Hayes, Janice, *Warrington History Tour* (Stroud: Amberley Publishing, 2018)

Hayes, Janice, *Warrington in 50 Buildings* (Stroud: Amberley Publishing, 2016)

Hayes, Janice, *Working Lives of Warrington* (Stroud: Amberley Publishing, 2011)

Pollard, Richard and Nikolaus Pevsner, *The Buildings of England: Lancashire, Liverpool and the South-West* (2006)

Wells, Harry, *Walking into Warrington's Past* (series)

Other Key Resources

Warrington Museum's galleries and its Archives & Local Studies collections

Acknowledgements

This book would not have been possible without the work of the many people who have contributed to and documented the story of Warrington. Particular thanks are due to the staff of Warrington Museum & Local Studies and Archives section and especially Philip Jeffs. All images are from the collections of Culture Warrington and every effort has been made to trace the copyright holders.